May I Have Your Order, Please?

How to Get What You Want From God

May I Have Your Order, Please?

How to Get What You Want From God

By
Pastor Rickie G. Rush

Black Pearl Publishing
Dallas, Texas

Published by Black Pearl Publishing
P.O. Box 222088
Dallas, Texas 75222

Cover design by Creative Matters

Manufactured in the United States of America
Library of Congress Data in Progress
ISBN 0-9667850-9-6

TABLE OF CONTENTS

Preface

I first met Pastor Rickie Rush when my late wife, Dorothy, brought him to our home. He was a student of my wife's and she was very fond of him. We didn't have any children, and she took a special interest in Rickie. He was only ten years old at the time, and had lost his mother. Over the years, he and my wife developed a unique bond, and he has become one of our spiritual sons. She thought a lot of him and saw great potential in him.

After spending a lot of time around Rickie, I knew exactly what my wife saw in him. There was no doubt that he was predestined to do something great. I was not surprised when he accepted the call to the ministry, because it was evident that God had gifted him in a unique way.

Over the years, I have had the pleasure of watching Pastor Rush evolve from a young man to a mentor of youth. His youthful energy is contagious and has enabled him to have one of the largest and most effective youth ministries in the Dallas Fort Worth area.

Pastor Rush is, without a doubt, one of the most creative pastors that I know. Through his theatrical background and his musical expertise, he has been able to create one of the most anointed worship experiences that I have ever seen.

Throughout the years, I have had an opportunity to watch him, counsel with him, and worship with him. He is most definitely a brilliant man who is developing a church model that should make others take notice.

Through the work he is doing at the Inspiring Body of Christ Church, Pastor Rush is setting an example for us on how to take our churches across age lines and class lines, which makes his ministry most effective.

There is no doubt that Pastor Rush is someone whom we all should emulate as God continues to exalt his efforts.

With his new book, _May I Have Your Order, Please?_ he is using his life experiences to serve up a tasty recipe of faith for the body of Christ.

Pastor Zan Wesley Holmes
Pastor Emeritus, of St. Luke Community United Methodist Church
Dallas, Texas

Foreword

I was very impressed when I first met Pastor Rickie Rush. His youthful and energetic personality is contagious. I was performing at his church one evening for a benefit concert. On my schedule, it stated that I was performing at IBOC. I kept thinking IBOC was some type of theater or auditorium. To my surprise, IBOC was the abbreviation for the Inspiring Body of Christ Church, which is a wonderful church led by a wonderful man.

I was warmly greeted and received by Pastor Rush and his enthusiastic congregation. It was easy for me to realize this was not just a meeting by chance, and I quickly developed a level of admiration and respect for Pastor Rush and his ministry.

Anyone who knows Pastor Rush realizes that he has a very cutting edge youthful perspective on dealing with ministry. His concepts have worked and have allowed him to develop a thriving ministry in the southern sector of the Dallas/Fort Worth Metroplex. We all know that success breeds success. Therefore, it is awesome that he is taking the principles that he has learned over the years to bless the body of Christ.

Those fortunate enough to read, _May I Have Your Order Please?,_ will be blessed. I pray they will apply the principles from this book, so that they can be a blessing to others as well. -

Vickie Winans

Dedication

"Everybody is somebody, even if nobody knows who you are."

This book is dedicated
to the memory of the mother who birthed me from love
(Rose Marie Gibson)

and the mother who raised me with love
(Mary Louise Rush)

Now they are both dwelling in heaven above.
God sent them here to fill His special order.
I'll never forget them.

Love,
Rickie Glen
(The Special Order)

"Therefore I say unto you, whatsoever things you desire, when you pray,
believe that you receive them, and you shall have them."
(Mark 11:24)

INTRODUCTION

When I first became a Christian years ago, it became readily apparent to me that there were people in the church who appeared to have everything – nice cars, clothes, and houses. And, it became equally apparent that there were those who seemed to have hardly anything.

In trying to figure out why some people had more than others, I began to ask questions like:

- Is God prejudiced?

- Does He love some of His children more than others?

- Do I need to do anything to become one of the ones He loves <u>more</u>?

Of course, the answer to all of the aforementioned questions is **NO**. And, today, having been grounded in Scripture, those questions seem a bit foolish to me now. My guess is that you may have asked yourself those same questions.

There is nothing wrong with questioning. In fact, questioning can be good because, as I sought answers to my questions on a personal level, it led me to a deeper walk with the Lord. That deeper walk ultimately gave me my answers, and reinforced my faith.

God wants all of us to be blessed. He wants all of us to walk in victory. He wants each of us to be vibrant, excited, and victorious in all areas of life. That is one of the things setting Christianity apart from mere religion.

When I finally came to that realization, I was determined to share this insight from God with the body of Christ in a way that all people could receive and understand it. The Holy Spirit led me to develop an easy-to-follow process that would guide people from the point of prayer to actually claiming and possessing the promises of God. So I can say without apology that the Holy Spirit compelled me to write this book.

The Lord revealed to me through the Holy Spirit that He did not want me to write just another book. His revelation to me was that He wanted me to create a tool to help believers reclaim their spiritual lives.

No book, of course, can replace the Bible. It is our manual for living the Christian life. But, there are times in our daily walk with the Lord when we need practical examples of how to apply spiritual principles for our daily survival in the world. Unfortunately for many Christians, life seems to be an ongoing process of simply trying to survive. It becomes a litany of going from day to day and from paycheck to paycheck. When that is the case, unbelievers look at Christians and do not see the victory they have experienced in Christ.

That is a shame, because Christians are not supposed to be normal as the world defines normal. God wants us to be joyous and victorious in all things – and the way we can do that is to claim His promises, to truly be heirs of Christ.

It should come as no surprise to you that many of those who struck it rich had to dig for it. It was not just handed to them. Obviously, there are people who are exceptions to this statement, but I am not talking about them. My reference is to people who may not have found what they needed right away. But, after continuing to go through the process, they found what they needed.

This book is God's way of simplifying the process for you. It gives you the tools to get what you want from God. Once you grasp these simple Biblical concepts, you will have them forever. No one can take them away from you.

Strange as it sounds, as I was contemplating how to present this material so it could be easily understood, I thanked God for allowing me to be poor. Having been poor in a material sense provided me with an understanding of how to prosper in a spiritual sense. This is something I might not have fully grasped had I been materially blessed throughout my life.

I now know this was positioning by God to provide me with an understanding of all that is necessary to help others to go through the process. After all, if you have never been caught in a downpour without an umbrella, you cannot describe or tell someone how it feels. This book is not a manual or an umbrella, but a step-by-step guide, hopefully, to lead you out of a stormy situation.

People who have seen and heard me preach are aware that I am a very demonstrative pastor. I spent several years in the Dallas Independent School District as a theatre arts instructor, and used dramatic presentations not only to help my students understand the arts, but to also get a clearer perspective of life. I have learned over the years that it is much easier for people to follow what they can see rather than what they hear. But if you can combine both seeing and hearing, there is a greater possibility that an individual will comprehend the point you are trying to make.

On any given Sunday you are likely to see anything in my pulpit from a football to a hat – practically anything that I can use to make a specific point. When I preach, I want to preach with clarity. And, the ultimate goal of every message I bring is to change lives.

My diverse congregation is indicative of the many lives that have been changed as a result of my breaking down messages in a way that people can easily understand. For me, it is important that everyone from preschool age to senior citizen get the message. I go out of my way to show practical examples to the congregation, so that they can easily understand how to apply the teachings to their everyday lives.

When the Holy Spirit first birthed in me the idea for this book, I taught a weeklong series at my church, which started on a Monday night.

On that first night, I had a cart with hot dogs – and all the fixings to go along with them – placed near the pulpit facing the congregation. I had ushers dressed in chef hats and aprons.

At the beginning of the service, I made an announcement for all the children in the audience to come down if they wanted a hot dog. You should have seen them rushing down the aisles! Everyone could smell the hot dogs in the hallway, so I knew this was a long-awaited opportunity for me.

Throughout that evening service, I used numerous examples to explain the principle of placing your order with God, but I never gave out the hot dogs.

You should have seen the long faces at the end of the service. Not one child got a hot dog. Needless to say, none of them were happy with me. Even my daughter was disappointed at the end of the service.

I continued to make the same appeal every night, but I never gave out the hot dogs. Each night the line for hot dogs got shorter and shorter.

I gave my final invitation to have a hot dog that Friday, the last night of the series. On this night, I did not have the hot dog cart come out, but again asked all the children in the congregation to come down to the altar if they wanted a hot dog.

By this time, I had a lot of angry people. Parents were mad at me, children were mad at me. My daughter would not even come down to the altar. Fewer children came down to the altar because they were afraid of being disappointed again.

But as I continued speaking, a few children did come down. And, before I began my message, I brought out a hot dog and handed it to a little girl who was about twelve years old. I then asked her to please give it to the child sitting next to her.

She never said a word; just handed it to the child next to her. She expressed no disappointment with my request. I then told her to sit down.

I had the remaining faithful children, those who had come down for the promise of a hot dog, escorted to a private room. On video monitors, the rest of the congregation was able to see the children escorted into a room full of hot dogs, with all the fixings, chips, and sodas they wanted.

These kids had waited patiently all week, and now they were getting more than they had ever anticipated – more than they had asked for.

All they wanted was a hot dog. All they thought they were getting were hot dogs and, maybe, some ketchup and mustard – because that is what they had seen earlier in the week.

The greater blessing was what they did not see.

By the end of the service, I could feel everyone's eyes on me. The girl who had waited all week and had given up her hot dog still had not gotten her order filled. I called her to the front and sat her in a large king-style chair. The ushers then brought in a table with a white linen cloth and set it before her.

As soon as she sat down, they carefully placed fine china and silverware on the table. They immediately formed a line, bringing in all kinds of foods that children love. I am not just talking about hot dogs, but chicken, hamburgers, and pizza. They kept bringing food and drinks, and then came the desserts. After she finished eating, we had a limousine pick her up and drive her through the community. The entire church watched the trip on our video monitors.

I had used this young lady and the children in our church to explain the principle of waiting in line for what God has in store for us. Even though I watched the line dwindle every night when the children were not getting their orders filled, I knew exactly when they were going to get the hot dogs.

And, when I asked that child to give up her hot dog, I knew she was going to get much more if she would just be obedient and give.

The same concept holds true with God. He knows when we are going to be blessed. If we can accept it, wait and not complain, we open the door for the greater blessings.

With this book, I am going to teach you, in a very fundamental way, how to get the Scriptural blessings that every Christian wants and has a right to receive. There are so many things God has for us. He does not need them. He has them for us, and our job is to get them from Heavenly places.

How do we do it?
We do it through the process of prayer. This book was written to show you how to use the power of prayer to turn your desires into reality.

What is prayer?
Simply put, prayer is communication or a conversation between you and God. Prayer is one of

the greatest privileges enjoyed by the children of God, and the benefits are immeasurable. It is through the process of prayer that we personalize our relationship with our Heavenly Father, because prayer breeds intimacy between God and His children.

Everyone who has entered into a personal relationship with Jesus Christ has the right to pray, and should pray. In order to live the kind of life that pleases God, we must develop a habit of talking to Him daily. God has made everything we can ever need or want available to us and prayer is the way to receive these things.

Basically, prayer is simply talking to God just like you would talk to your very best friend. God cares deeply about each and every one of our problems and is just waiting for us to come to Him with those problems. The Bible tells us over and over to constantly bring our problems to our Heavenly Father.

Prayer is not to inform God of something He may not be aware of, or to try to convince Him to love us more. He already knows our needs and He has certainly shown His love for us. Prayer's purpose is to assist us in building our relationship with God. It is that intimacy that breeds our blessing.

Also, prayer should never be a monologue, but rather a dialogue. There are always two people involved in a prayer (conversation) – you and God. So be prepared for God to speak to you, and when He does, He wants you to listen.

Prayer unleashes God's power so that He is able to work on our behalf. It opens the channels of God's blessings.

Prayer is the tool God uses to accomplish the things that He wants to see happen in our lives. Prayer opens new doors of opportunity for God. Prayer is like a door, with Jesus standing on the other side waiting for us to ask Him to grant us the desires of our hearts. When we pray, it is like turning the knob to that door and swinging it wide open.

And, when it comes to prayer, we must remember that we are responsible for three things: having faith in God, obeying His Word, and waiting patiently.

When we pray, we are giving God permission to step into our lives. God has limited His power in our lives to the importance that we place on prayer. Even when we do not see anything significant occurring, God is still at work solving our problems. When it appears that there are no answers, God is there waiting for the proper time to give us the solution.

If this is true, you may ask, "Why do so many Christians never get answers to their prayers?"

"Why do so many not get what they want?"

Well, there are many reasons. Sometimes we are afraid to ask God for things because of our circumstances. For example, you may desire a new car, but your job pays only five dollars an hour. A new car is available to you -- even at five dollars an hour, but what God has to do first is change the conditions around you.

The problem is not that God does not answer our prayers, but that we have not been taught that there is a process between praying and receiving.

By the time you finish this book, you will be ready to receive all that God has for you. I want you to get the same message in your spirit that our congregation got from our teaching series. The best way to do this is to use examples from everyday life that you can easily understand.

In the minute-to-minute society in which we live, we are used to getting everything quickly. This is true even in the way we get our prepared meals. Some of us go out for breakfast, some for lunch, and others for dinner. At some point during our week, the majority of us visit a fast food restaurant with a drive-through window.

Over the next few pages, I am going to use this principle to empower you to get all that God has for you. In the following chapters, I will break down concepts of enriching your prayer life: selecting from the menu, placing your order, pulling up to the window, paying for your order, what to do while waiting in line, and why special orders take more time.

As you go through your own personal drive-through window of life, it is time to place your order. Before you turn this page, I want you to think about whatever it is you really want from God. What is it that you have been waiting for all of your life? What is the one thing you have always wanted that seems bigger than life? Just imagine pulling up to the window and seeing God

there waiting to serve you. He has one simple question:
May I Have Your Order, Please?

"My concept for Williams Chicken grew out of a need in our community. I had a genuine concern for young men in the neighborhood. I wanted to create a company that would be an example to help at least one kid get off drugs, or find another way of life other than the streets. I have followed Pastor Rush for years, and admired his example and his work with young people. I am intrigued with his philosophy, because it parallels with my reason for being in business."

Hiawatha Williams
Owner of Williams Fried Chicken
Dallas, Texas

Chapter One
SELECTING FROM THE MENU
(The Fun Part of Life)

"Be not therefore like unto them: for your Father
knoweth what things you have need of before you ask
Him." (Matthew 6:8)

Everyone has to realize that at some point in life
you have to make choices from the menu of life. There
comes a point where you sit down and realize that you
really are allowed to dream. You are allowed to
explore the full potential of your imagination.

This is what I call the fun part of life. It is full of
possibilities and unlimited resources. There is no
penalty for allowing your imagination to run wild. You
are allowed to say to yourself, "One of these days, I am
going to feed hundreds of people on the street."

Or, "One of these days, I am going to have a Mercedes-Benz."

Or, "One of these days I am going to own a nice home."

You can dream of getting married, having children, or going to a far-off country. Whatever your imagination can comprehend, you can dream.

The Scripture says:

"Delight yourself in the Lord and He will give you the desires of your heart." (Psalm 37:4)

David, who penned those words, knew a lot about dreaming – and about dreams coming true. He was a man who spent a lot of time talking to God, allowing God to see the full extent of his emotions, and venting his frustrations to God. If the Psalms teach us anything, they teach us that you can talk to God about anything and everything that is on your heart.

David's dialogue with God was not just praise. He uttered plenty of gripes and complaints, too, because he knew God was listening. He was quite aware that God knew everything that was going on in his life, but did not expect God to *act unless he asked.*

Those who desire God must pursue Him. And, David did plenty of that. God, obviously, truly enjoys those who include Him in everything they do because, despite all David's blemishes and sins, it is written that he was a man after God's own heart. I would love to have that written about me, and anyone who would not relish such a platitude needs to do some self-examination about his or her relationship with the Lord.

Knowing God enables you to understand His menu for your life. God must be sought in order to be experienced. Delighting (taking pleasure in, appreciating, enjoying) yourself in knowing God through reading His Word (the Bible) helps you to understand His menu for your life.

Unfortunately, most people are not spending much time in the Word nowadays, so they have not even found the menu. They excuse their lack of Bible study with being "too busy." However, they are not too busy to plop down on the couch and spend three and a half hours watching a ball game on television. Or, they are not too busy to spend an hour or two on the telephone gossiping about a brother or sister.

The truth is that people will make time for what they think is important, and too few people who call themselves Christians give the Bible the importance it deserves in their lives. Plenty of brothers can quote chapter and verse of the NFL (National Football League) and NBA (National Basketball Association) Rule Books, but they do not know one thing about the only Rule Book that counts – the Holy Bible. Until you get acquainted with that Rule Book, you are not going to know what is on the menu.

It is God who places desires inside you, but in order for you to know that, you must know Him and His Word. And you must talk (pray) to Him daily.

In a natural father-child relationship, the child sees the father as someone he is not afraid of and someone he respects and loves. The father is looked up to and, most of all, he is attainable and approachable. No appointments, no scheduling, no waiting in line to get to him. It is easy to reach him and to talk to him.

Can you imagine having to make an appointment to talk to your natural father? I guess certain circumstances might make that necessary -- a father's job -- but I think you will agree that the necessity of such scheduling would be highly unusual for most of us. In fact, most kids do not mind interrupting their dad – no matter what he is doing – nor do they mind asking him for what they want. Of course, fathers and mothers have to weigh what a child wants against what he or she needs.

If you know the Bible, you realize that when you were born God knew everything you were going to need, but He also knew there were some things you were going to want. When you ask God for a house, car, job, or maybe just peace of mind – He has it to give. God already has for you everything that you could ever ask God for.

So, maybe you are wondering, "Where is it?"

With God.

"Where is God?" In Heaven.

Many people have no idea what they can receive from God.

Why?

It is because they do not know the Word. They live their entire lives going without, and they die never having experienced the abundant life promised in God's Word.

If the abundant life for you means getting a new car, you need to know that it is available to you. If it means a three-story house, or new clothes, these things are available to you.

Many people do not realize this because they do not understand that it is God's desire for them to have nice things. God's desire is for *His children* to have the best of everything. Just because you cannot find a reference in your Bible for a Mercedes-Benz, a new house, or a spouse, does not mean these things are not included in "the Book." There is, in fact, a Scripture that describes all of the things I just mentioned – and even more. There is even a Scripture that assures us that, as children of God, all of the spiritual and material goods we desire from God are available to us.

Jesus said:

"Therefore I say unto you, whatsoever things you desire, when you pray, believe that you receive them, and you shall have them." (Mark 11:24)

Now, read this Scripture again, and make it personal, putting your name in the parentheses:

"Therefore, I say to you, (your name), whatsoever things you desire, when you pray, believe that you will receive them and you shall have them."

First, let's look at the word *"desire."*

A desire is a longing or a hunger for something. So the question is: what do you desire right now? The first step to getting your prayer answered is that you must have a desire.

I used to think that I had to wait until God gave me what He wanted me to have, but that is contrary to the Word of God. According to Mark 11:24, it is whatever I desire.

Now, take a minute and think about all the things you desire right now. No matter what they are, the Word of God calls them *"whatsoever things."*

The world may call it a promotion, but to God it is a "whatsoever thing."

The world may label it a new house or car, but to God it is a *"whatsoever thing."*

Maybe you need healing in your body. To God, that is no problem – it is only a *"whatsoever thing."*

The term *"whatsoever things"* means anything you want from God. And, we serve a God who specializes in *"whatsoever things."*

There are no limits to what we can ask God for – and there are no limits to what we can receive. If you desire it, you can have it, and proper prayer is the way to receive it.

So, where do the desires of our heart come from?

They come from God.

God wants you to know that it is His desire to add to your life. You just need to ask Him.

"God is able to do exceedingly, abundantly above all that we ask, according to the power that works in us." (Ephesians 3:20)

What you desire is already in you, but it must be called forth (spoken out loud). Remember that God answers prayers, not thoughts. To pray is audible (sound), but thinking is not. Thinking carries no weight, and it does not need a response or answer from anyone because it is not heard.

If you trust God and you love God, He will place within you the desire for what He is going to give you. God will cause you to desire the things that you thought you made up yourself.

What will be already is.

Before you were born, God had a purpose for you and your life, and everything that you were ever going to need had been included in the plan. Scripture reminds us just how special we are to God and how, before we were born or even formed in the belly of our mothers, God knew us.

"Before I formed you in the belly I knew you; and before you came forth out of the womb I sanctified you." (Jeremiah 1:5)

Now, that is awesome!

The Lord loves you so much that He will have you thinking about a pink Mercedes-Benz, or something crazy like that. Out of nowhere you may think, "I want a pink Mercedes-Benz!" You may even wonder where the thought came from, not realizing that God actually gave it to you. The idea could never come to you without God first placing it there. You could never dream it, or think it, or speak it, without first having had the internal desire.

Designing our purpose is up to God.

Fulfilling our purpose is up to us.

It is said that faith without works is dead. God wants to hear from you. Whatever you want from God, you must ask Him for it. No one else knows what you want – only you.

For example, imagine a large, ice-cold glass of Pepsi. The glass is almost full to the top. The ice in the glass is slowly melting. The outside of the glass drips with moisture and is covered with frost. Now, all of a sudden, you find yourself getting thirsty.

What is the first thing you want to drink?

You want a Pepsi, of course, because I painted a visual picture that caused you to think about Pepsi, even though it might not have crossed your mind until I used my oral paintbrush! Pepsi may not even be your favorite drink but, because of the picture I painted in your mind, you now have the desire to drink a Pepsi. All you can think of is that, when you get out of church, or when you leave work, the first thing you want to do is get an ice-cold Pepsi to drink.

Although I originally created the desire in your mind by painting a vivid oral picture for you, it was your own mind that began to actively see the picture, and it was your own senses that caused you to want an ice-cold Pepsi. And, you really will not be satisfied until you get that Pepsi. Water will not fill that thirst, tea will not fill that thirst, and no other soft drink will fill that thirst. No matter what you may get to drink, you will continue to go back to that original picture of an ice-cold Pepsi that I painted in your mind.

Exploring the things we desire is definitely a fun part of life. No matter where you are in life, whether a teenager or senior citizen, such exploration is enjoyable. Most of us like to dream, to think of the endless possibilities if only those dreams would come true. What many Christians fail to realize is that those dreams can come true – if they will but select from the menu that is in the Bible.

There is always great anticipation when looking at a menu board full of items from which you can make a selection. The primary thing we have to learn as Christians is that the Bible is our menu board. It is exciting to be able to go to the Bible and to make selections from the menu God has prepared for us.

In order to make this as simple as we can, we will pretend that a drive-through restaurant represents Heavenly places. For example, a McDonald's or a Burger King.

When you drive up to the restaurant, the first thing you see is a menu, right? And, what is normally on the menu? Everything that they have inside. When you became a Christian, God already had a menu available for you called the Bible. The Bible is God's itemized menu of promises.

In our menu, we discover there are many promises stored up for us, and available for the asking. In God's Word we find there is peace for confused minds, power for the faint, joy for those who mourn, and praise for heaviness of heart. There are an unlimited number of promises in God's Word, yet many Christians continue to live defeated lives because they have never learned how to acquire those promises. Pure and simple, they have never learned to operate by faith.

Faith always gets God's attention.

The writer of Hebrews states it as follows:

"Now faith is the substance of things hoped for, the evidence of things not seen." (Hebrews 11:1)

Faith is telling God, "I believe and trust in Your Word." Regardless of the consequences or circumstances before you, faith is obeying and trusting God, no matter what.

Genuine faith moves a person from mediocrity to greatness in God's eyes. It replaces stagnation with hope. It gives a person a shovel with which to dig out of his or her hole of complacency, and instills passion and enthusiasm for reading and understanding God's Word. Real faith causes God to smile with approval – and what more could a Christian want than the Father's approval?

It is, obviously, important for believers to both know and understand the menu.

Have you ever been to a restaurant and ordered something, got it and asked, "What is this?" The problem was that you did not know what you ordered, because you did not understand the menu.

Just hearing the Word is not enough to know the menu. You must go on to meditate on it day and night – until you are confident, convicted, and convinced that God *can* and *will* do exactly what He says He is going to do in His Word.

In other words, God's Word must begin to shine in your heart, and not just ring in your ears. In order to grow to this level of maturity, you must learn to "abide" in the Word.

Jesus said:

> "*If you abide in Me, and My words abide in you, you can ask anything in My name and I will give it to you.*" (John 15:7)

Let your perception become your reality. Perception is insight, awareness and even observation. It is letting what your faith truly is come into clear focus.

Here is the promise, and God does not break promises:

> "*If you abide in Me, and My words abide in you, you can ask anything in My name and I will give it to you.*"

The "*anything*" is your perception – your faith. It is what you are asking for and wanting so much that you can almost taste it, hear it, and even touch it. You become unmovable in your trust in God because you believe that He has heard you, and now you are anticipating the manifestation, or response to your desire.

It is important to point out that God's promise is conditional on certain things. The first condition is: "*If you abide in Me.*"

What does it mean to abide?

Well, to abide means to remain, stay, or take up residence. In this Scripture, Jesus says:

"If you remain, or live in Me, and my Word remains, or lives in you, you can ask anything in My name and I will give it to you."

The important thing to note here is that the Word will not get into you until you get into the Word. Wanting to know God and His promises is up to you. It does not come about by osmosis. It takes an act of commitment on your part – studying and learning the Scriptures. And, that commitment comes from prayer and listening to the Holy Spirit, who Jesus said would guide you in all things.

As followers of Christ, we abide, or remain in Him, by reading the Word daily and consistently submitting ourselves to do what the Word commands us to do. If we do this, then we can be assured that when we pray we will receive whatever we ask of God.

To abide in Christ is to renounce any independent life of our own, to give up trying to think our thoughts, or to cultivate our feelings, and to simply and constantly rely on Christ to think His thoughts in us, and to form His purposes in us. Again, that is possible when you allow Christ, through the Holy Spirit, to direct every aspect of your life.

Paul put it very succinctly:

"Let this mind be in you which was also in Christ Jesus." (Philippians 2:5)

If that is not letting it all hang out, I do not know what is!

But, back to Jesus' conditional statement, a part of which is: *"And My words abide in you."*

If we are to receive from God all that we ask from Him, we must study His words, let them sink into our thoughts and into our hearts, keep them in our memories, obey them constantly in our lives, let them shape and mold our daily living and every act. By meeting both conditions of this Scripture, abiding in Him and allowing His Word to abide in us, we can stand confident knowing that when we ask – we will receive.

Can we do it?

Of course we can.

Paul wrote:

"...being confident of this very thing, that He who has begun a good work in you will complete it until the day of Jesus Christ." (Philippians 1:6)

This Scripture means that when you let God control your life, He is going to keep on doing it until Jesus returns. And, when Jesus does come for you, with what God has in store for you in Heaven, you are not going to be wanting, or needing, any earthly stuff. Our finite minds cannot come close to comprehending what He has waiting for us in Heaven. What we have here – even a Mercedes-Benz – is like leftovers at a dollar store compared to what we are going to have in Heaven.

We arrive at the menu, and a voice comes over the intercom and asks, "May I have your order, please?"

Who said that?

What is that person's name?

Do you know him or her?

Can you see him or her?

No, you cannot see the order taker. And, no, you probably do not know him or her. But, you respond to the voice because you believe that he or she can hear you.

Well, praying to God is the same way. You cannot see Him, but you trust and believe that when you ask for what you want in prayer, He is going to fill your order.

Now, you may ask, "Pastor Rush, Do I need to pray for the same thing over and over?"

Well, we need to look at that question in a logical manner. Suppose you are at a McDonald's and you drive up to the menu and order station, where you place your order for a Big Mac and fries. You might want to add a Coke, too, or a Diet Coke. And you might ask the order taker to make sure to include extra catsup and salt. And, after placing your order you do something strange.

You do not drive to the pickup window. Instead, you drive past the pickup window, go around the block, come back to the menu and order station, and repeat the order you had already made earlier to the voice that asks, "May I take your order, please?"

Then, again, you do the same strange thing. You bypass the pickup window, go around the block, come back to the menu and order station, and repeat your order.

You do the same strange thing again. You drive right past the pickup window, go around the block, come back to the menu and order station, and repeat your order. You follow this same procedure over and over again. And, the question is: why?

Do you distrust the person taking your order? Do you think he or she is ignoring it?

I am sure you get my drift here – that eventually you need to realize that your order has been received, and that now all that is required of you is to wait patiently for it.

If you believe – have faith – that your order was received the first time, why would you need to ask again? The order taker got your order the first time you placed it, so you do not have to keep repeating it.

Likewise, God hears your prayer the first time you pray. You must have the confidence to know He has received your prayer and will give you the desires of your heart.

John wrote:

"And this is the confidence that we have in Him, that, if we ask anything according to His will, He hears us: And if we know that He hears us, whatever we ask, we know that we have the petitions that we desire of Him." (I John 5:15)

"Ask anything" sounds a whole lot like *"whatsoever things you desire."*

Notice what this verse *does not* say. It does not say that we know that we are going to get it. It says, *"We know that we have it."*

What does *"know"* mean?

To *know* something means it is an absolute fact; that there is no debate and no argument. In other words, it is a done deal.

So now, we need to get real.

After careful review of the menu, you place your order. Maybe you order a Big Mac with no sauce, fries with no salt, and a chocolate shake. The voice of the order taker says, "That will be five dollars and ninety-five cents. Drive to the first window, please."

You have made your desire known; you have placed your order.

And, you have now been instructed to pull up to the first window.

This is important. In fact, it is critical. To get your order filled, you must do what you are asked to do. All you have to do is stay in line and keep your desire.

Pretty easy, right?

Now be warned, you may stay in line waiting on the manifestation of a prayer for many years, but do not get discouraged. Rejoice in knowing that the manifestation of your blessing is on the way.

Some people may ask you why you are still waiting, and even remind you that you have been waiting a long time. But, you can tell them that because you have placed your order, according to Jesus' own words in Mark 11:24, you have it.

Praying with Specificity

Another question people often ask is, "How will I know that God has answered my prayers?" My reply: "Is it what you asked for?"

In other words, did you pray with specificity? Did you ask for a car, or did you ask for a new car right off the showroom floor with leather seats, a sunroof, and CD player?

That is called specificity.

Specificity can be defined as great detail. The prayers of Christians are often too general, so the individual praying becomes confused as to whether his or her prayer is answered. That is why it is critical that you pray with specificity.

If you pray with specificity, you will always know exactly what you have asked for – and you will also know when, or whether, it is God who has answered. When God answers prayers, it will add to your life and not take away.

For example, if God blesses you with a new car, you will not have to sacrifice your tithes and offerings to pay your car note. Always remember that:

> "*The blessings of God maketh rich and addeth no sorrow.*" (Proverbs 10:22)

At some point in life, everybody will eventually come back to this first chapter, because it is the fun part of life. Sometimes we get so busy that we may actually forget what we ordered. Therefore, it is important to check out the menu board again. By doing this, some of you may realize that you have already received what you ordered, and others of you may realize that you must continue to wait for God to fill your order.

Chapter Two
PLACING YOUR ORDER
(The Easy Part of Life)

Chapter One dealt with the fun part of life, and practically everybody I know likes to have fun. However, this chapter deals with placing your order, which is *really* the easiest part of life.

We can all say what we want – that is easy. But, sometimes people say things and do not really mean them, or do not understand the power of the words they are using. That is why it is so easy. To speak does not take a lot of thought. It does not take a lot of preparation. All you have to do is open your mouth.

That can be a problem, especially when one's tongue becomes a tool of the devil. But, we are talking about something altogether different here.

Just imagine that you are walking in the mall, or down an aisle at Wal-Mart. As you saunter along, you are thinking to yourself, "I want this," or "I want that."

If you actually told a Wal-Mart associate what you wanted, he or she would be more than happy to get it for you.

That, obviously, is easy.

Likewise, naming your *need* calls it forth from the spiritual realm. Being specific removes all doubt.

It is okay to simply say what you want, and to daydream about all the things you would like to accomplish. It does not impact anyone because you are just thinking it, not speaking it. But, the Bible says we can have what we say.

Jesus said:

"For verily I say unto you, That whosoever shall say unto this mountain, Be thou removed, and be thou cast into the sea; and shall not doubt in his heart, but shall believe that those things which he saith shall come to pass; he shall have whatsoever he saith." (Mark 11:23)

We need to realize and understand that words are powerful. Even though they may be easy to use, they speak to our very destiny. Our words determine what we may actually receive in life, because through Christ we have access to unbelievable richness.

Just think about the ease with which you can place an order at a McDonald's. You simply drive up and say, "I want a Big Mac with fries and a chocolate shake."

It is easy to tell that unseen person exactly what you want. It requires practically no effort. All you do is open your mouth and let the words spill out.

And, you have faith that an unknown person whom you cannot see is going to do exactly what you ask.

A lot of people want God to do specific things for them, but they are afraid to open their mouths. They want to go before God, but they are afraid to tell Him exactly what they want.

Let me give you some very sound advice. Do not let anyone, or anything, stop you from bringing your need to Jesus. When you diligently seek God, He will "hook you up."

But, you have to speak to God. You have to commit yourself verbally to saying, "God, this is what I want." You cannot go to God and wimp out. You have to make your request known.

Paul wrote:

"Be anxious for nothing, but in everything by prayer and supplication, with thanksgiving, let your requests be made known to God." (Philippians 4:6)

When you are placing an order, you have to speak up – not mumble incoherently or vacillate about what you want. Check the menu and know exactly what you want before even starting to place an order. If you start wavering and cannot make up your mind, you are not ready to place an order. You are holding up the line.

So when you go to God with an order, know exactly what you want. God does not want a wishy-washy prayer request, He wants something specific. He wants to clearly understand what you want so that He can fill your order.

If you drive up to the menu board at a McDonald's and just stare at it, you are not going to get anything. That voice that asks, "May I take your order, please?" is not a mind reader. God, of course, does know what is on your mind, but He has told you in His Word that He is only going to act on your desires if you ask for His intervention.

If you are at a McDonald's and expect to get what you want, you have to speak up. You are not going to get your order filled by just thinking about it. It does not matter how much money you have, or how much education you have, you are not going to get a thing if you drive up to the menu board and just look at it.

The same holds true with God. If you just look at what you want and do not ask Him for it, nothing is going to happen. For me, the easiest part of the entire process is speaking my desire.

Of course, I speak a lot and do not have the slightest difficulty telling God what I want. I do not feel awkward talking to God and asking Him for things because I talk to Him all the time. Talking to God is not unusual for me; it is as normal as a sunrise.

But, I understand if it is not that easy for you. I do want you to know that it can be if you will simply cultivate your relationship with God. He is always willing to listen to you, and you do not have to be an articulate, glib speaker to voice your wants and needs to Him. Just be who you are. Do not spend a lot of time trying to phrase things just right. If you ask God, He will even help you with the words to say, but it is not so much what you say as what is in your heart. He wants love from you – and honesty. You cannot lie to Him and get away with it, so you might as well tell Him what is on your mind.

Have you ever gotten in trouble because you knew what you wanted to say, but you could not find the right words to say it? That can be a problem for some brothers and sisters. At some point, you just might want to associate with people who can help you find the right words to say.

Some of you might find yourselves getting into trouble because you have "great thoughts" in your mind, but when it comes time to transfer those thoughts into words you mess up.

For example, a guy is thinking about walking up to a girl and saying, "I would like to get to know you."

But, in his attempt to express what he is thinking, he instead walks up to her, stumbles over his words, and says, "I want to get with you." His thoughts and words do not coincide, so the girl's perception comes from what he is saying and not what he is thinking. All he initially wanted to know was the girl's name, but his spoken words gave her a totally different view of him. Now, she not only does not want to give him her name, she does not want to ever see him again. His opportunity to get to know this young lady vanishes because of the words he speaks.

Let's face it – he blew it! His mind told him the right words to say, but his mind and mouth were not in harmony. That is a problem for many Christians. A person's mind tells him or her the proper thing to say, but his or her mouth gets them into trouble. To live a victorious Christian life, everything has to be in sync – heart, mind, soul, and body. We need to make sure that what we think and say is properly understood.

Because I want to make sure that I am conveying a ministry message that will reach everyone, I often surround myself with teenagers. They help me keep up with the current phrases and lingo that young people are using. Putting thought and oral expression into a package that everyone can understand is critical in ministry. Satan wants to confuse us, and what better way can he do this than by aiding people in misunderstanding the Word of God? Scripture is always clear, but the way some people interpret it is not.

Sometimes teenagers get upset with their parents because their parents do not understand the terminology they are using. We have to realize that, over the years, meanings and words change, and there are often gaps between language and meaning. For example, in the English language we do not use "thee" and "thou" any longer, except in the reading of the King James Version of the Bible. There are, in fact, many words in the King James Version of the Bible that we no longer use in conversation. But, we know what the words mean, and we understand that language evolves over a period of time to provide a better understanding of our environment.

We now live in an age of technology, which has spawned many new words that would have been alien to our ancestors. Teenagers today know and understand computer terminology that many of us cannot comprehend. These kids grew up with computers and terminology that may seem like a foreign language to many of us.

But, it all comes back to words – and how we use them.

Your words can reveal your innermost desires. Many people might look at your words as confessions and immediately think of negative things. But, a confession can be a positive statement. The Christian life is actually full of positive confessions. Some Christians do not experience successful Christian living because they have not been taught how to achieve it.

In the past, you may have tried to achieve successful living by becoming involved with social and civic organizations, or by being a member of a church for a long time. But, that is not the key to successful Christian living.

The key to success is seeing the good in every situation.

Every Christian is capable of receiving what he or she needs and wants from God based on his or her confession. Every time you speak, something happens in the spirit realm.

If you do not say anything, nothing happens. If you do say something, something will happen.

God is more than able to supply you with abundance, but He needs something from you. God has to have your spoken words in order to work on your behalf.

If, when you pray, you get on your knees and just "think" about what you want God to do, and you do not say anything, you are just thinking. It is important to know that if God does not hear anything, He cannot supply anything.

Have you ever wondered why God gave human beings a mouth?

He did not have to.

He gave us mouths because He wants to hear from us. God does not want to spend His time translating our thoughts. He wants to converse and commune with us, and that requires some effort on our parts.

The bottom line is that God answers prayers, not thoughts.

God knows your thoughts, but do you really want God to answer every one of your thoughts?

I do not think so.

We think a lot of things that we do not want God to answer, and that is why we must make positive, oral confessions. And, when you make confessions with your mouth, make sure they are positive confessions.

If you form a habit of saying negative things, even if you do not mean them, you will have some negative circumstances. We have formed such a common habit of saying negative things that we often apply the negative to the positive things we really want to say, and we end up getting the wrong results.

Before I became wise to the devil's schemes, I would unknowingly make negative confessions and would sometimes advertise the devil in my attitude and on my face. But, once I learned I was a champion and a victor, even though situations in my life felt like they were tearing me apart, I would begin to make positive confessions, just the opposite of whatever I was feeling.

Sometimes with tears in my eyes, I would confess, "I'm a champion." And, before I knew it, I would begin to feel like one.

That is why it is extremely important that you are properly taught the Word of God. You cannot operate in what you do not know, and what you do not know may be the difference between life and death for you or a member of your family.

Satan gets very nervous when we as Christians know our rights in Christ and begin to confess them. He does not care that you go to some musical or spend your money going to some Gospel play. That is great, that is good entertainment, but it does not change lives.

What you need in order to lead a successful life in Christ is a daily diet of the Word of God. In order to win against the devil, knowledge of God's Word is essential – and once you know it, you must confess it. It is impossible to have joy in difficult times without knowing Christ.

The power of positive confessions is also good, but not good enough for us to achieve the level of living

God desires for us. You see, thinking positively is always better than thinking negatively – and it will put you in a better frame of mind for dealing with the negative things happening to you. But, you must begin to make positive confessions from your mouth. In other words, the power of positive confession in line with God's Word will change everything. What we must begin to do is say things that will reinforce the positive thoughts that we have, then we can develop a habit of saying positive things.

Be assured, your circumstance – no matter what it may be – is not beyond God's ability. And, if you do not want the negatives, you had better stop saying the negatives.

For example, if you were to say, "Every time she comes around she makes me sick," that is called a negative confession. When we make negative confessions, Satan is listening and makes sure that the person who makes you sick shows up every time, because you confessed it with your mouth. You brought it to pass in your life.

See how powerful confession is?

When you make negative confessions with your mouth, you cause "negative manifestations" to come from the Spirit world into the physical world – and this does not happen until you say it with your mouth. The word "manifestation" means to bring to sight, or make available to the senses. When something is manifested, it means that it is tangible or that you can see, taste, touch, smell, or hear it.

When we make positive confessions, it manifests, or brings into sight, the blessings of God in our lives. That is why we must be careful as to what we confess with our mouths at all times. Remember, when you make a negative confession, Satan will take your words and use them against you in the same way God takes your positive confession and uses it for your good. God answers prayers, and Satan answers complaints.

Be Careful as to What You Hear

The promise of a long life is for those who hear and receive God's sayings. Hearing is tied directly into receiving the promises of God. Once you get filled with God's Word, it slows down the dying process.

> *"Blessed is the man that hears me; watching daily at My gates, waiting at My post and My doors."* (Proverbs 8:34)

This Scripture tells us that God's blessings are always a result of true hearing. If you hear, you can be blessed.

What does *"blessed"* mean?

Blessed means empowered to prosper. God has put something in you to cause you to go farther. As God's child, you have been given the power to prosper. And, real prosperity deals with a lot more than money. It involves both abundance and peace, and significant increases in every area of your life.

Prosperity is the power to control your circumstances instead of your circumstances controlling you. Hearing the Word of God gives you that kind of power.   The things that you lend your ears to will determine whether you are a victor or victim.

When Satan tries to put sickness on you and whispers in your ear, "You are going to die from this," you have to drive the devil and his lying symptoms right out of your life. The key to overcoming any sickness and poverty is continually hearing the Word of God. It empowers you to take control over any demonic influence that may be trying to overtake you.

You have to take control of your situation with the Word of God. If you spend time listening to your doctor's bad reports and the stories from your relatives about all the people in your family who died, you might as well go ahead and plan your funeral.

Do not believe those negative reports. Confess what God says about your situation. Guard your ears because what you hear is extremely important. Your mouth will begin speaking what has been sown into your heart through the gateway of your ears.

A friend in the ministry and I were enjoying a barbeque dinner at a popular restaurant. I had not paid any attention to the fact that there was an old jukebox in the place, or that it was providing a steady diet of songs. The music was simply background noise to us. We had not seen each other for a long time, so we continued to talk long after we had finished eating.

On the way to our cars, without even consciously thinking about it, we both started singing one of the lyrics from a song that had been playing on the jukebox. We were shocked by the fact that this song had taken up residence in the subconscious of both of us.

During the time we were talking, we did not think we were paying any attention to this music, but the music, obviously, penetrated our spirits. Here we were, two men of God, saturated in the Word of God, but these lyrics had somehow worked their way into our spirits simply because we had heard them in the background.

Can you imagine what the music our children hear over and over does to their spirits? Music that degrades women, uplifts drug usage, and glamorizes gangster lifestyles is harmful to the spirit. And, this type of music is pervasive in today's world. It is almost impossible to filter out, but we have to try.

What you hear is very important. It is difficult to overstate just how important a part hearing plays in your spiritual life. Your ears are one of two gateways into your spirit. The two ways of entering your spirit are through your ears and eyes.

Satan knows that whatever you receive in this world spiritually is either going to come through your eyes or through your ears. Hearing, obviously, is a direct link to your faith. Just remember that the devil cannot make you do anything. He can only suggest. Therefore, you must accept responsibility for controlling your own thoughts.

Hearing is nothing more than receiving through your ears. But, the "hearing" referred to in the Bible involves a little bit more than that. It requires attentiveness, which means you need to pay attention while you are hearing. It involves obedience and belief. There is no great secret to handling the situation. Whatever you feed will grow. Everything you starve will die.

Paul wrote:

> *"How then shall they call on Him whom they have not believed? And how shall they believe in Him of whom they have not heard? And how shall they hear without a preacher? And how shall they preach unless they are sent? As it is written: 'How beautiful are the feet of those who preach the gospel of peace, who bring glad tidings of good things.' But they have not all obeyed the gospel. For Isaiah says, 'Lord, who has believed our report?' So then faith comes by hearing and hearing by the word of God"* (Romans 10:14-17).

Verse 14 discusses calling on God when you never knew He was available to call on. This introduces an important spiritual truth. You cannot believe in, or ask for, something that you have never heard preached.

Have you ever noticed that where salvation is never preached, nobody gets saved? People simply go to church and focus on politics, social events, and community issues. Maybe they hear a lot of good stuff, but if what they hear is not centered in the salvation experience, nobody gives his or her life to Christ.

Sometimes salvation is preached – "You need to be saved" – but healing is never preached. So people are saved, but nobody ever gets healed – and many are sick all the time.

The bottom line is that you cannot have faith in something you have never heard. That is why it is so important that teachers, preachers, and evangelists all share the entire truth of the Word of God, from A to Z.

If you are sick and you need faith to get healed, then faith comes by hearing the Word of God concerning that healing. It does no good to hear the Word concerning finances if you have cancer. It does not help you to hear the Word on healing if you need rent money. You need to hear a Word from God concerning *your specific situation* in order to acquire the faith needed *to receive your blessing.*

Whatever you desire comes from hearing and acting on the Word.

God has a Word, or message, that specifically deals with your particular need. It is important to understand that faith does not come from having heard. Faith comes from hearing – and hearing is present tense. Faith is based on the knowledge of God's Word. And, life without faith is foolish.

Hearing and Believing

If the number of times something is repeated in a Scripture is any indication of its importance, then we need to be sure that we learn the lesson taught by Jesus in this Scripture:

> *"For verily I SAY unto you, whosoever shall SAY unto this mountain, 'Be thou removed, and be thou cast into the sea'; and shall not doubt in his heart, but shall BELIEVE that those things which he*

*SAYS shall come to pass, he shall have whatever he
SAYS. Therefore, I SAY unto you, whatsoever things
you desire when you pray BELIEVE that you
receive them and you shall have them"* (Mark
11:23-24).

Note that "believe" is mentioned twice, while "say"
is mentioned five times. The ratio between "saying" and
"believing" is five to two. Could this mean that Jesus
knew we would have a harder time with the *saying* than
with the *believing*?

Possibly.

But, regardless as to what you have been taught or
led to believe up until now, God's way of operating by
faith is for us to *say it* first, then we will *see it*. Positive
confession works if you believe it is going to come to
pass. Therefore, walk like you believe God's got it.

God has already told us that whatever we desire
from Him we shall have, but if we cannot conceive it in
our minds and confess it with our mouths, we will
never receive it in our hands. For some reason,
unfortunately, we have greater confidence in words
spoken by man than in words spoken by God. We tend
to think that man is always going to do as he promises,
and act as if we cannot count on God's promises. But,
God has given us an entire Bible filled with promises,
all available to us just for the asking.

The Scripture says, *"For verily I say unto you,
WHOSOEVER..."* It does not say, "Whosoever is a
Christian," "Whosoever is a preacher," or "Whosoever
has been a member of a particular church." It just says,
"Whosoever shall say."

Did you know that you are a "Whosoever?"

He is talking about you, making reference to you. The Scripture says, *"Whosoever shall say"* – not hope, dream, or think – but *"Whosoever shall say."*

Get the point?

As a Christian you must learn to "*say*" or "*confess*" with your mouth. Whether positive or negative, we will *have it* if we *believe it* and if we *say it.* We receive what we say if we confess it and believe it and receive it in our hearts.

We have God's Word on it.

I wish I could say that this only applies to Christians, but Mark 11:23 is a Spiritual law, and that means it will work for you whether you are a saint or a sinner. As long as you function inside the law, it is going to work for you. A sinner can say, "I'm going to have a good day, " and he or she will have a good day. He or she can say, "I'm not going to let anything bother me today. I do not care what happens, nothing is going to bother me." And, he or she will have the kind of day they say they will have. The importance of what you say cannot be overstated.

The Gospel of Mark reads:

"Then, they came to the town of Jericho. As Jesus was leaving there with His followers and a large crowd, a blind beggar named Bartimaeus (son of Timaeus) was sitting by the road. He heard that Jesus from Nazareth was walking by. The blind man cried out, 'Jesus, Son of David, please help

me.' Many people scolded the blind man and told him to be quiet. But He shouted more and more, 'Son of David, please help me.' Jesus stopped and said, 'Tell the man to come here.' The blind man stood up quickly. He left his coat there and went to Jesus. Jesus asked him, 'What do you want me to do for you?' The blind man answered, 'Teacher, I want to see you again.' Jesus said unto him, 'Go thy way; thy faith hath made thee whole.' And immediately he received his sight, and followed Jesus in the way" (Mark 10:46-52).

In this story we see the plight of a blind beggar by the name of Bartimaeus sitting on the side of the road. Being blind, Bartimaeus, obviously, never witnessed the many miracles Jesus had worked, but he had "heard" about them. On hearing that Jesus was coming to town, he made a decision to act on what he heard. In his hopeless condition, he began to cry out as Jesus was passing by.

Though Bartimaeus had no physical sight, through the eyes of his faith he believed that Jesus could heal and make him whole. As a result of Bartimaeus' blind faith, Jesus called him over and restored his sight. Bartimaeus acted on what he heard and received a miracle.

The same thing can happen to you. It happens time and time again – over and over. When you act on what God's Word tells you to do, when you speak out to God in faith and ask for a miracle, you will receive it.

If you say, "Well, I'm going to try this and see if it works," do not expect a miracle because what you are expressing is not real faith. You do not have to put God through a battery of tests to see if He makes a passing score. God has already knocked the top off every test we have ever given Him. God has nothing to prove, but you do. Your test is whether you will do exactly what He told you to do to receive a blessing.

If you study the Word, you understand that in Scripture the vinedresser is the keeper of the vineyard, or watchman over the field. Some people might think his interest in the field is only in the spring, when he can be seen planting the seeds, or at harvest time, when he is reaping the crop. He might spend other months during the year helping clear a neighbor's rocky field, or helping someone build a new house. He could, of course, watch and worry about the vineyard every day and night of the year – about pestilence, droughts, famine, and the scorching hot east winds – but he knows God controls these things.

What the vinedresser has learned over time is the secret of patience. He has done what he was supposed to do, and then he must depend on the power of God, through nature, to bring the crops to fruition. The invaluable secret he teaches us is, "to let go and let God" do His thing.

We need to be patient, and we should not be negative – worrying about events and circumstances beyond our control. We need to have faith and patience, to not be anxious, but to understand that God sees the end from the beginning.

We need to have the wisdom to know when to plant and when to sow, when to hold on and when to let go, when to undertake new tasks and when to let God bring them to completion.

When a person can do that, he or she is well on the way to being the kind of person God wants him or her to be.

E.M. Bounds, a great preacher in both the nineteenth and twentieth centuries, wrote in his book *Power Through Prayer,* "It is true that Bible prayers in word and print are short, but the praying men of the Bible were with God through many a sweet and holy wrestling hour. They won by few words but long waiting. The prayers Moses records may be short, but Moses prayed to God with fasting and mighty crying for forty days and nights.

"The statement of Elijah's praying may be condensed to a few brief paragraphs, but doubtless Elijah, who when 'praying he prayed,' spent many hours of fiery struggle and lofty [discourse] with God before he could, with assured boldness, say to Ahab, 'There shall not be dew nor rain these years but according to my word.'

"The verbal brief of Paul's prayers is short, but Paul 'prayed day and night exceedingly.'

"The 'Lord's Prayer' is a divine epitome for infant lips, but the man Jesus Christ prayed many an all-night before His work was done; and His all-night and long-sustained devotions gave to His work its finish and perfection, and to His character the fullness and glory of its divinity."

In the same book, called by many "the greatest book on prayer ever written," Reverend Bounds also wrote:

"Hurried devotions make weak faith, feeble convictions, and questionable piety."

But, one of his strongest statements – one we should all commit to memory – is that "To be little with God is to be little for God."

Chapter Three
WHAT'S AROUND THE CORNER?
(The Tricky Part of Life)

Assume now that you have looked at the menu board, and have placed your order. Placing your order is an exciting part of the drive-through process, but now comes what can be a very tricky part of life – trying to determine what is around the corner.

Because you are behind other cars, you cannot always see what is ahead of you – except for the rear end of that car immediately in front of you. So you move up ever so slightly in line and the wait begins. It may not be all that long, but it seems like an eternity.

And, we have all been in a situation where, once you pass the menu board, there is a quick turn before you pay for your order at a window. Sometimes, if you are not paying close attention, before you make that turn you almost run into the building!

There are a lot of things in life just like that tricky, sharp-edged turn. There are hard-to-negotiate things like unforgiveness, unconfessed sin, fear, improper motives, lack of knowledge, and a lack of love – all of which help abort our orders before we even get to the first window. And, even if your order is not completely aborted, it may slow down the process of God getting your blessing to you.

This is the easiest time to "get out of line," because you and others have placed special orders with God – and those orders are going to take a little time. So the journey you were once excited about is now becoming very frustrating. Though the wait is becoming longer, you are required to believe your order has been taken and that it is being filled. This is a time when you cannot see anything happening, but you have to believe -- have faith -- that you are going to receive what you have spoken to God about.

If you want victory in God, you must keep your eyes on the unseen. Spiritually speaking, you must develop the art of waiting on God.

There are some who think patience is the ability to wait. Actually, patience is a fruit of the Spirit, and it comes forth *while* you are waiting. Patience involves how you act while waiting, because it is during this time that your character is being developed. You are experiencing the process of God's timing. In other words, this is the one time in your life when you are not operating the remote control of your life.

You brothers know how hard it is to give up the remote control for the TV! You want to keep a firm grip on it because you want to watch the football game and she wants to watch a love story on the Lifetime Channel. In fact, you want to watch all the football games, so you keep switching from channel to channel. And, she just sits there getting madder by the minute. Do not act as if you do not know what I'm talking about, because this is an example practically everyone understands!

Well, if you want God's blessing in your life, you are not going to be in control. You have to tune in to God's channel and stay there. You cannot keep clicking to other channels and expect His blessing. You have to hand the remote control to God

Some of you have become tempted to stop waiting on God and have tried to answer your prayer on your own – or you have become willing to settle for something less than what you asked for. This comes as no surprise. It is Satan's way of knocking you off balance, and his way of trying to destroy what should be your focus.

When you try to answer your prayer yourself, you are going out on a limb alone. That is because what God initiates, He sustains. What you initiate, you have to maintain. You cannot do anything well without God's constant help. When you run ahead of God and try to answer your prayer on your own, the enemy is making a fool of you.

Settling for something less than what you have asked for is destructive to your faith because you never experience what it is like to fully trust God through the faith process. You cannot place God on your personal timetable and expect Him to do exactly what you want Him to do exactly when you want it done. Think about it: if you received everything you wanted from God at the exact time that you wanted it, you would be in a big mess right now. In fact, there would then be no reason for you to exercise your faith at all.

There are some things you are asking God for that you are simply not ready to receive. You should be grateful that God follows His plan, not yours.

The maturing of your character, increasing your finances, and being Spirit-led are a few of the many areas in your life that God wants to fix before some of the other blessings He has for you can be manifested. Going on ahead, doing it your way without God is the sure path to failure. He may bring your blessings about in one week, one month, one year, or even ten years, but you must not doubt what He has promised.

Abraham was the father of faith, but he was guilty of listening to his wife, Sarah, and of not waiting for God to fulfill His promise that they would have a son in their old age. Abraham and Sarah took it upon themselves to fulfill God's promise, so Sarah provided her husband with a surrogate to fulfill the promise of God. So Abraham produced a son with Sarah's handmaiden instead of with his wife, and this son, Ishmael, was not the son of promise.

When Abraham changed God's plans, he brought great sorrow into his and Sarah's lives. But, we tend to forget that what was done was also hurtful to Ishmael and his mother. This couple's lack of patience in waiting for God to fulfill his promise caused all kinds of problems – and those problems were not confined to them alone. Our impatience with God is often devastating to other people, including loved ones and friends.

Later, of course, Abraham and Sarah did have Isaac, their son of promise, thus God's promise to them was fulfilled. But why was there ever any doubt that God would do exactly as He promised?

God will provide. He will fill our order. He does not need our help, but He does expect your patience – which is the key element of real faith and trust.

Note that God did not interfere with Abraham's decision to have a son with Sarah's handmaiden, and He even blessed Ishmael, but only because he was Abraham's son. The true inherited blessings and fulfillment of the promise only came through Isaac.

God will not interfere when you make the decision to go ahead of Him and try to answer your own prayer, but you will end up with an *Ishmael blessing* instead of your promised *Isaac blessing*. For example, you may end up with a husband or wife, but not a man or woman of God. You may end up with a car, but not the new one God had lined up for you.

While you are waiting in line, you will see others "pass you by" as they purchase houses, get married, get divorced, get married again, have children, begin new careers, start new businesses, and so on. Do not worry about all that – your order is on the way to being filled because you are waiting on God.

You should not even speculate as to whether those other brothers and sisters waited on God, because your order is an individual thing – it is between you and your Heavenly Father. There is one thing you can count on during your wait. You will receive renewed strength, because God provides it when you are in His *wait mode*.

Always remember this verse:

"But those who wait on the Lord shall renew their strength; they shall mount up with wings like eagles, they shall run and not be weary, they shall walk and not faint." (Isaiah 40:31)

This is a beautiful Scripture. Looking to the strong, muscular eagle, the Biblical writer describes his all-powerful God. The eagle has long been a symbol to Biblical writers, and it is uplifting to know that God will bear us *"on eagles' wings."* (Exodus 19:4)

Think about the swiftness of eagles. They can fly at a speed of eighty miles per hour, so God is telling us that with His help we can be swift and mighty – and that we can conquer the things that try to keep us from being all we can be in Him. In fact, God's care and comfort for His people is often likened to a mother eagle's care for her young. The eagle's nest is secure and virtually inaccessible to predators. Mountain climbers who have come close to an eagle's nest can tell you a thing or two about the fury of a mother eagle protecting her home.

With wingspans from nine to ten feet, the eagle encompasses her young to keep them from harm. The psalmist compares God's care for His people to the eagle's wings.

> *"Hide me under the shadow of Your wings."*
> (Psalm 17:8)

What do you do while waiting for your order to be filled? Look to God for an eagle-powered faith. Prepare yourself by waiting patiently for your dreams. And, when God gives them to you, let them soar to new heights of reality.

Productive waiting involves expecting delays, and not getting bent out of shape by them. If there are delays when you are waiting on God, there are always reasons for them – and God may not be the reason. You might be causing the delay, or another possibility is that Satan is causing it.

You should never think of God's delay in bringing about your blessing as a "No." It is, instead, orchestrated for divine appointments in your life. Remember that God knows your life's path from beginning to end, so learning to trust Him totally is the key. On your journey to receiving what you have asked from God, His plan for your life is still in motion. You can know your delay is from God when you are still receiving favor from Him while you are waiting.

Satan's delays are meant to hinder you from actually ever receiving anything from God. They are designed to frustrate your faith and cause you to be upset with God. Satan knows that if you become upset with God, you will not be in God's presence. The enemy hindered the apostles on their mission, so no believer is immune to this type of attack.

Take this Scripture to heart in your quest to serve God:

> *"Some trust in chariots, and some in horses; but we will remember the name of the Lord our God."* (Psalm 20:7)

The power of the name of Jesus is as real in our lives as it was in the early Church. When we place our trust in Him, we have access to the greatest power in the universe. Some people take pride in the fact that they work for a large company, in their family name, or in some title they have. But, as Christians we come in the name of the Supreme Authority. We come in the name of the Lord. And, we have that promise He gave us, *"Whatsoever you ask in prayer, believing, you will receive."* (Matthew 21:22)

And, also remember these words of Jesus:

> *"And nothing will be impossible for you."* (Matthew 17:20)

You could very well be personally responsible for the delay of your blessing. Have you sown seeds of doubt instead of faith?

> *"Thus says the Lord of hosts:* 'Consider your ways!'" (Haggai 1:7)

This is serious instruction. Planting into God's system of seedtime and harvest time (tithes and offerings) provides a guaranteed harvest. Not giving into God's system is like putting your money into a sack with a hole in it. You must learn to trust God with your substance or money.

Haggai is a poignant, hard-hitting, straight-to-the-point, no-questions-asked book of the Bible that encourages people to get started and to never quit. This book was written after Israel's exile from Babylon, and Haggai was about eighty years old at the time. But he motivated the people to believe in themselves and to undertake the task of rebuilding the temple.

As you can well imagine, he was faced with innumerable negative thinkers who imagined every excuse possible for not rebuilding the temple. They said they should wait for the right time to begin, for the necessary funds, and for the large amount of people and material necessary for the task.

It is possible that Haggai saw the temple in all its glory before its destruction. The longer you live, the more stuff you see – good and bad. But, the important thing is that he was motivated to encourage the people because he had a vision of what they could do with their time, talents, and ability if only they applied themselves.

Haggai told these brothers and sisters that they did not have a material problem; they had a motivational problem. They did not have a money problem; they had an idea problem. They only needed to do two things to be successful – to get started and to never quit.

Postponing tough decisions is, more often than not, the result of a lack of faith. God promises to bless us when we make a commitment to live and walk by faith. We expect God to bless our lives and professions when we stop doing nothing and start doing something.

That needs to be repeated. We expect God to bless our lives and professions when we stop doing nothing and start doing something.

When we decide to begin, the biggest problem is solved. Beginning is half the battle.

The enemy is constantly trying to prevent you from ever receiving your order. Many things can happen during your wait: divorce, death of a relative or friend, early pregnancy, job loss, and any number of other things. These things are designed to get you off focus so you will "get out of line" and give up on God and your prayer.

It is critical that you keep focused on your destination instead of the situations you encounter along the way. The very situation the devil uses to break you down is what God uses to build you up. Going through a divorce, death, unexpected pregnancy, job loss, or any other difficult life issue is your opportunity to be strengthened by God to "press through." You must remember that you are not what you are *going* through, but what you have *come* through. Your adversity is unique because God has entrusted to you a measure of adversity that only you can handle. It is God who gives you strength from the inside, which enables you to override what you feel and what is happening to you.

While you are waiting on God, surround yourself with positive people and things. Let friends and family members who share and appreciate what you are doing in your life encourage you. Do not be discouraged by those who do not see the good in what you are going.

And, do not curse your hard times. These are the times that will usher in your next victory. You can be joyful in tough times by being destination-driven, covenant-conscious, and faith-filled.

It can be difficult to keep your destination in focus while hard times come at you, but this is how you will soar above your adversity. In Numbers 23:19 we are told to remember: *"God is not a man that He should lie."*

Remembering that God has made promises to you keeps your belief and faith intact, because God always honors His Word. Every believer has been given a measure of faith from God:

> *"For I say, through the grace given to me, to everyone who is among you, not to think of himself more highly than he ought to think, but to think soberly, as God has dealt to each one a measure of faith."* (Romans 12:3)

So you must continue to get filled with God's Word so you can be filled with faith. There is absolutely no situation you face that is beyond God's ability.

Once you place your order with God, believe that He is working on it. Whatever you do, do not get out of line. Here are some things that can be around the corner that you never expected, and that can cause a delay in your receiving your blessings:

- ◆ Unforgiveness

- ◆ Unconfessed Sin

- ◆ Improper Motives

- ◆ Fear

- ◆ Lack of Knowledge

- ◆ Lack of Love for Others

When you pray, you must be sure that there are no obstacles to getting your prayers answered. Believe it or not, Satan can carefully orchestrate events to stop the flow of your blessings. If you are ignorant of such obstacles, you may think God is saying "No," when He is really saying, "Yes, but wait."

The main obstacle to your faith is the devil. He is not fighting you because of who you are, but because of where you are going. He's terrified of where you are headed. He heard you place your order and now he knows that you are on the way to having your order filled. Remember: it is the devil's mission to abort God's purpose and plan for your life.

Unforgiveness

A major tool the devil uses to help us abort our destiny is to cause us to walk in unforgiveness. There is always somebody who has done you wrong, talked about you, misused you, or told you they would be there for you and they were not. Now you are not able to forgive them and, as a result, you are stopping the flow of your blessing. God heard you place your order. In fact, He already had it coming your way, but there is this blockage keeping it from getting to you.

"And when you stand praying, forgive, if you have anything against any: that your Father also

which is in heaven may forgive you your trespasses." (Mark 11:25)

"For if you forgive men their trespasses, your heavenly Father will also forgive you: but if you forgive not men their trespasses, neither will your Father forgive your trespasses." (Matthew 6:14-15)

"Then Peter came to Him and said, 'Lord, how often shall my brother sin against me, and I forgive him? Seven times?' Jesus said to him, 'I say to you, not until seventy times, but until seventy times seven.'" (Matthew 18:21-22)

Is there someone who has made you angry?

Forgive them.

Unforgiveness will block your faith and abort your prayer. In Mark 11:25, Jesus says, "When you stand praying, forgive."

What do you do when you finish praying?

Do you forgive?

If you do not forgive, do not pray.

If you are not going to forgive, do not pray another prayer. If you are going to pray, you must forgive first. If you are not going to forgive, get up off your knees and do something else.

If I were having trouble getting my prayers answered, the first place I would check would be under unforgiveness. You should ask God, "Lord, am I holding a grudge against anybody?"

That is what I do. If I am having a problem getting my prayers answered. I check that out first.

Jesus said, "And when you stand praying, forgive."

This is not a suggestion; it is a command. He said, "ask and it shall be given unto you," but there is a condition attached to the statement. That condition is that you must forgive.

Some people fake forgiveness by saying, "I forgive them, but I cannot forget what they did."

That is like running in the rain with a hole in your umbrella. You are in the ballpark, but you will never hit a homerun. You must make a decision to forgive the offense and treat the person as if it never happened. You cannot continue to harbor negative memories of the past. You have to truly release the person before you become bitter about the situation. You must make the decision to forgive and move forward. You may never receive an apology, or give an apology, but you must forgive.

Unforgiveness is like a knot in a water hose that prevents the flow of God's blessing to you. As Christians, we must immediately forgive anyone who has wronged us in any way. Just remember that the cost of not forgiving is far too high. When you are hesitant to forgive others, think of the astronomical amount of times God has forgiven you. Give others mercy as you have received mercy. Unforgiveness is a device used by Satan to prevent the flow of God's blessings from reaching you.

Unconfessed Sin

The Scripture says:

> *"If I regard iniquity in my heart, the Lord will not hear."* (Psalm 66:18)

If there is sin in your heart when you pray, chances are you will not receive anything from God. We must continuously ask for God's forgiveness each day to assure a clear path to God and not hinder our blessings. We must be honest enough to admit when we have sinned and immediately ask God for forgiveness. The Word of God says that if we ask for forgiveness, God is faithful and just to forgive us and cleanse us from all unrighteousness.

Some people may tell you that one sin is greater than another sin. This is not true. Stealing is just as wrong as telling a lie to God. It is direct disobedience to His Word. That is why we must renew our minds daily with God's Word.

Unconfessed sin is like having your toilet back up. If you have things clogging up your sewer line, you will not be able to flush your waste. Flush your spirit daily by asking God to forgive you of your sins.

If you are a Christian and do not ask God's forgiveness, you will experience guilt. If left alone, guilt can become insomnia, angry outbursts, free-floating anxiety, criticism of others, and even physical disease. The good news of the Gospel is that God's forgiveness is a bigger event than your guilt.

The Bible presents an extreme case of guilt in the life of David.

"Blessed is he whose transgression is forgiven, whose sin is covered. Blessed is the man to whom the Lord does not impute iniquity, and in whose spirit there is no guile. When I kept silent my bones grew old through my groaning all the day long. For day and night Your hand was heavy upon me; my vitality was turned into the drought of summer." (Psalm 32:1-5)

God, of course, can deal with anything. Guilt is overcome if you tell it like it is (confess your sins) and turn to Jesus Christ as your advocate.

We prove that we are not too smart when we deny, hide, refuse, or cover up before God, as if He cannot possibly know what is in our minds. Relief comes from telling it to God just like it is – without embellishment or glossing over the truth. David took a shot at it. He spent a year in silence – speechless and mute before God. But, when he came to himself he made a threefold confession. We can learn a lot from his confession.

First, *Godwardly*, we have rebelled. The word "transgressions" means rebellion, revolt, or acts of sedition against the government of God. From a secular standpoint the word refers to a break in relationship between two parties. For example, David broke God's laws, violated his own conscience, and betrayed other people. When you look at David in that context, you see a pretty weak individual. But, he was able to turn things around when he related that guilt to God, not to other people, and asked forgiveness.

Second, *manwardly*, we have missed the mark. It is easy to miss the goal for your own life if you are too pigheaded to admit your sin and ask God for forgiveness. It is easy to have your aim deflected and to err from your own standards in life. The shepherd boy David never intended to do what the King David did. He would not have written Psalm 32 if he had not missed the mark set for his own life.

Third, *inwardly*, there is something that needs to be straightened out. We often rebel at the level of doing and miss the mark. That is not the biggest problem, or deepest truth, about us. Because of our unwillingness to confess our sins to God and ask forgiveness, there is something within us that needs to be set straight. There is something warped that needs to be unwarped.

David had to admit what he was, not just what he did. And, we must admit what we are, not just what we have done.

The moment we make this three-dimensional confession, we experience the pardon of God – but those in whose spirit there is no deceit must make the confession sincerely.

Here is another truth as it relates to unconfessed sin: guilt will deal with you if you do not deal with guilt. Three thousand years ago David made it clear that psychologically and physically guilt would have destroyed him had he not told it to God like it was.

Psychologically, guilt makes the conscience roar. David wrote that his conscience was *"roaring...all day long."* His conscience roared like a lion, as will your conscience if you refuse to confess your sins to God.

Do not, under any circumstances, confess them to me – or to some brother or sister who is going to tell all. Confess them to God.

Physically, guilt can affect the body. David wrote, *"When I kept silent, my bones wasted away."* Unconfessed sin (and guilt) can be devastating to one's physical health. David wrote that the framework of his body was racked, shaken, and that the seat of his strength seemed to disintegrate. He was fatigued and listless with no sense of direction or purpose.

There is no doubt that guilt extracts a great price in human thought and physical life. It can make a person self-destructive in ways he or she cannot understand. The answer: deal with guilt before guilt deals with you.

Of course, we know something better than David knew. He looked back to animal sacrifices and a temple. We can look back to Calvary and a Risen Lord, who is now our great Advocate.

We have an Advocate *presently*. Jesus, our Advocate at the right hand of the Father in Heaven, is immediately available to help us. Whether our sin was twenty years ago or yesterday, He is ready to provide forgiveness if we just ask.

We have an Advocate *positionally*. Jesus is face-to-face with the Father on our behalf, whereas our sin would shut us out from the presence of the Holy One.

We have an Advocate *powerfully*. He is the sinless Christ, which enables Him to stand in the Father's presence as our substitute.

"My little children, these things I write to you, that you may not sin. And if anyone sins, we have an Advocate with the Father, Jesus Christ the righteous." (1 John 2:1)

Improper Motives

"What causes fights and quarrels among you? Do not they come from your desires that battle within you? You want something but do not get it. You kill and covet, but you cannot have what you want. You quarrel and fight. You do not have, because you do not ask God. When you ask, you do not receive, because you ask with wrong motives, that you may spend what you get on your pleasures." (James 4:1-3)

Why do you want the things you want? Are there any ulterior motives in your heart? Many times we do not receive because we have the wrong motives in our hearts. We ask for things according to the lust of the flesh and not those things that would bring glory to the Father.

In the book of James, we read of Christians being rebuked by James. He admonished them because they were praying for the wrong things with the wrong motives. Because of this, their prayers returned empty. Such prayers never reach the heart of God and cannot, therefore, be answered. God, in all His goodness, is not going to answer these requests. God chooses to give us only those things that testify of His goodness and His favor toward us, and bring glory to His name.

James, the half-brother of Jesus, wrote the most practical of all the Epistles, demonstrating that love and Christian faith must be shared through works and deeds. It encourages faith to be lived out by sharing and helping one another. James also encourages his readers to stand fast in the face of trials.

For example, he wrote:

"My brethren, count it all joy when you fall into various trials, knowing that the testing of your faith produces patience. But let patience have its perfect work, that you may be perfect and complete, lacking nothing. If any of you lacks wisdom, let him ask of God, who gives to all liberally and without reproach, and it will be given to him." (James 1:2-5)

Again, we see that word "patience." It is a tough concept in a world that wants everything right now, but the Christian life requires that we exercise patience. Even in a fast food line, you do not get your order instantly.

James must have witnessed his brother Jesus' attitude of concern for those who were in need. Perhaps this is why he appeals to us not to be simply hearers of the Word, but doers of the Word by caring for the poor, visiting the sick and depressed, and helping widows. We should be a light of hope when others are going through tough times.

An attitude of acceptance is also needed toward those who have not lived up to their faith. James encourages us not to judge but to welcome them back with loving kindness. Much like his brother who touched the lives of all people, James tell us to be like Jesus – to find a need and fill it, to find a hurt and heal it. If we do that, we can chase off any wrong motives we have in asking God for our blessing.

Here is a hypothetical, but often true, situation. Your neighbor who never enters a church, or gives a dime to God's work, receives a promotion and big raise. You go to church three times a week, and support God's work sacrificially, but you were passed over for a promotion.

Maybe you have a coworker who laughs at God and ridicules your faith, yet he or she is as healthy as a horse. You live for God and you are sick all the time.

These undeniable realities can become the seedbed of doubt about God's existence or goodness if your motivation for serving Him is wrong. It is like placing your order, then having doubt as to whether the person at the other end of the speaker took your order. You begin to think that you may be in line for nothing – and that is exactly what Satan wants you to think.

Psalm 73 speaks to the tragedy of the wicked, and the blessedness of trust in God. It answers every doubt.

"Truly God is good to Israel, to such as are pure in heart. But as for me, my feet had almost stumbled; my steps had nearly slipped. For I was envious of the boastful, when I saw the prosperity of wicked." (Psalm 73:1-3)

It is natural to question the prosperity of the wicked, but spending your time doing so robs you of blessings. Because God gave us free will, there has always been injustice in the world. But, focusing on that instead of trusting in God is an exercise in futility. It will get you absolutely nowhere.

> *"For there are no pangs in their death, but their strength is firm. They are not in trouble as other men, nor are they plagued like other men. Therefore pride serves as their necklace; violence covers them like a garment. Their eyes bulge with abundance; they have more than heart could wish. They scoff and speak wickedly concerning oppression; they speak loftily. They set their mouth against the heavens. And their tongue walks through the earth."* (Psalm 73:4-9)

One of the great dangers to spiritual fulfillment is class envy. It seems as if these people who have it all do not even feel the pangs of death. They do not know trouble and the things that cause problems for most of us do not plague them. They are full of pride and arrogance because they have such abundance. They "mouth off" about all their earthly possessions.

If your motivation in praying for your blessing is to be like one of these folks, you have a real problem. Jesus told us that people like these already have their reward. They may walk proud and boastful in this life, but our stay here is very temporary compared to eternity – and then they have to pay the price for their arrogance. So you had better get your heart right and start laying up treasures in Heaven where they do not rust and decay.

What I'm saying here is that you are wasting time if you are envying what somebody else has. You are in line and you have placed your order. Be joyful about what God has prepared for you – because He prepared that blessing specifically for you, nobody else.

> *"Therefore his people return here, and waters of a full cup are drained by them. And they say, 'How does God know? And is there knowledge in the Most High?' Behold these are the ungodly, who are always at ease; they increase in riches. Surely I have cleansed my heart in vain, and washed my hands in innocence. For all day long I have been plagued, and chastened every morning."* (Psalm 73:10-14)

The psalmist is feeling sorry for himself here, which is the attitude a lot of brothers and sisters have when they do not get an immediate response from God. They do not want to stay in line for their blessing; they want to cut ahead of somebody and get in front of the line.

But, this Scripture has to do with evil folks having more than good folks, and the psalmist is complaining to God about it. Now take a good look at how he achieves a measure of understanding about his lot in life compared to that of those who already have an abundance of material possessions.

> *"If I had said, 'I will speak thus,' behold, I would have been untrue to the generation of Your children. When I thought how to understand this, it was too painful for me – until I went into the sanctuary of God; then I understood their end."* (Psalm 73:15-17)

The man is finally getting his act together here. And, how does he do that? He goes into the sanctuary of God. He goes to church.

If you want God's blessing, you need to get into God's Word and you need to get into church. I'm not talking about just attending; I'm talking about genuinely becoming a part of the body of Christ. When you do that, your attitude will get right. You will not spend your time worrying about what somebody else has. You will focus on your blessing and what God wants you to do for His kingdom.

After you hear what the man says about these people who already have theirs, and who are boastful and arrogant about their material possessions, all envy toward them should depart from your heart.

"Surely You set them in slippery places; You cast them down to destruction. Oh, how they are brought to desolation, as in a moment! They are utterly consumed with terrors, as a dream when one awakes. So, Lord, when You awake, You shall despise their image." (Psalm 73:18-20)

Now, having read those verses, how many of you would like to trade places with the folks who have everything on earth but God? Brothers and sisters who question whether there is a hell need to take a real close look at these verses.

In the next verses the psalmist starts apologizing to God for his doubts, which is a good lesson to all of us.

"Thus my heart was grieved, and I was vexed in my mind. I was so foolish and ignorant; I was like

a beast before You. Nevertheless I am continually with You; You hold me by my right hand. You will guide me with Your counsel, and afterward receive me to glory. Who have I in Heaven but You? And there is none upon earth that I desire besides You. My flesh and my heart fail; but God is the strength of my heart and my portion forever. For indeed, those who are far from You shall perish; You have destroyed all those who desert You for harlotry. But it is good for me to draw near to God; I have put my trust in the Lord God, that I may declare all Your works." (Psalm 73:21-28)

We can learn a lot from this psalm about *finding the faith that defeats doubt.* We learn, among other things, that *doubt springs from the observation of life.*

Your *reaction* to life may cut the ground out from under your faith. Godless people do pretty well in the world, and that bothers many Christians. You may even feel envy when you see their prosperity.

This comes from the *observation* of life. Unbelievers do prosper. *Outwardly*, they seem to be exempt from the struggles of ordinary people. *Physically*, their bodies are sleek, strong, and stylish. *Inwardly*, their "fat hearts" look through evil eyes and their mind is a fountain that never ceases to flow with selfish schemes. *Verbally*, they speak as if they were gods in their own world, acting as if the whole earth belongs to them and disparaging everything and everybody.

Their popularity galls many Christians and leads them to the desperate conclusion that it does not pay to serve God. This is especially true of people who put more emphasis on material possessions than on spiritual insight. Believe me, you are going to get the blessing you prayed for if you stay in line, remain patient, and trust God.

Granted, there are people who waltz from success to success without God – but you do not want to be in their number. The end of this life for them is not a pretty thing.

Restoration of faith *begins* with our influence on God's people. Just remember that other Christians and unbelievers are looking at you, and just think about how any cynicism and doubt on your part might affect them. Jesus handed you the ball and pointed you toward the end zone, and if you trust Him nobody can stop you from scoring your blessing.

Restoration of faith *happens* when we meet God. Trying to solve the mystery of why unbelievers are having success in this life when you are not can be a real dilemma until you take the problem to God. You find the answers to your questions in the Word and in God's house. This is where you can get your value system reversed; where you discover that the wealth, glitter, and pompous attitude of the ungodly is but a vapor that passes quickly away.

Restoration of faith *leads* to confession. *Negatively*, we may think more like a beast than a person. Sometimes we have to confess that we react with no more faith than a whining coyote – until we get our values reversed and quit groveling in the negative.

Positively, it is necessary to affirm some things about God and one's self. God is present even in our doubts. And, He protects us and provides direction when we are about to slip.

When we are in the Spirit, the thought of God fills every horizon in our life. He is all we want in Heaven or on earth. Our raging, doubting ego disappears and our superficial evaluation of the godless vanishes. We have our place in line for His blessing and we are not going to lose it.

Fear

"And He said unto them, 'Why are you fearful, O ye of little faith?' Then He rose and rebuked the winds and the sea; and there was a great calm." (Matthew 26:8)

Satan will steal your peace of mind if you begin to worry and fret about things happening to you. Fear knocks at the door, faith answers, and fear flees. When fear comes in, faith automatically goes out. Fear and faith cannot occupy the same space. Until you exercise your faith, fear is going to stay. But when faith is inside, fear cannot penetrate. Our faith acts like a shield to protect us.

"The Lord is my light and my salvation; whom shall I fear? The Lord is the strength of my life; of whom shall I be afraid? When the wicked come against me to eat my flesh, my enemies and foes, they stumbled and fell. Though an army should encamp against me, my heart shall not fear; though war should rise against me, in this I will be

confident. One thing I have desired of the Lord; that will I seek: that I may dwell in the house of the Lord all the days of my life, to behold the beauty of the Lord, and to inquire in His temple. For in the time of trouble He shall hide me in His pavilion; to the secret place of His tabernacle He shall hide me; He shall set me high upon a rock. And now my head shall be lifted up above my enemies all around me; therefore I will offer sacrifices of joy in His tabernacle; I will sing, yes, I will sing praises to the Lord." (Psalm 27:1-6)

The psalmist faced the choice of faith or fear, and this psalm expresses a tried faith that triumphed in spite of very real fears. Your personal faith can overcome fear when God dominates your life.

Faith overcomes fear when God is first. You must begin with faith or fear will flourish. The psalmist affirms that God is light, salvation, and safety – and because of the priority of his praise, fear can find no place in his life. God is light that dispels darkness and leads the way out. God is rescue in the face of all that chases him, and a stronghold in view of all that endangers him. His dependence is exclusively on God. He has given up any dependence on other people or himself.

Faith overcomes fear when faith is personal. The faith of the psalmist is intensely personal. He did not overcome fear through understanding theology or by remembering only what God had done for Abraham and Moses. God is a triple shield to him only in the personal character of his faith. Brothers and sisters, faith that is personal overcomes fear.

Faith overcomes fear when we remember past experiences. Most of us can remember how faith overcame our fears in the past. That knowledge strengthens us. The psalmist remembered how his faith had triumphed over actual threats. People with intense personal ill will had tried to devour him with vicious speech. In each instance they had stumbled and fallen.

Think about it: most of the bad things you thought would happen did not happen, did they?

The fearlessness of your faith will depend on the singleness of your desire. The psalmist looks into the future and at the past and says with confidence that one thing pervades his life – a desire to commune with God. This singleness of heart provides peacefulness of heart.

Fearless faith desires communion with God. The psalmist desired always to be in God's house.

How about you?

The psalmist desired an intimate, inward fellowship with God. Constant communion of that nature renews fearless faith. For us this means being both localized and spiritualized. It means being in the place where God's people meet when they meet – and it means we commune with God even when we are away from that place.

Fearless faith involves contemplation of God, something that many Christians do not practice. But, like the psalmist, we should desire an extraordinary experience of God. Like David, we should desire to *"behold the beauty of the Lord."*

When your desire is to see through all the acts of worship to the reality behind them in the face of God, when you earnestly mark everything in the worship service for what is revealed about God, your faith will become fearless in your communion with and contemplation of God.

Personal faith also gives a hiding place. When your faith in Him is personal, God will habitually hide you from enemies and elevate you above difficulties. God is our host and protector, and gives us a sheltering asylum from danger. Remember what Paul wrote: *"In all these things we are more than conquerors through Him who loved us."* (Romans 8:37)

We must be aware that fear is a design of Satan and that God will allow anything you will allow. If we are going to talk about faith, then we have to look at who is fighting against us. The force of evil steals, kills, and destroys. If you let him, Satan will steal your faith, your hope, your dreams, your laughter, your joy, and anything else you carelessly make available to him. He will use anything and everything, anyone and everyone, to keep you from filling and receiving your order.

Lack of Knowledge

"My people are destroyed for lack of knowledge: because you have rejected knowledge, I will also reject you, that you shall be no priest to me: seeing as how you have forgotten the law of your God, I will also forget your children." (Hosea 4:6)

When you lose contact with God's Word, you lose contact with your faith. If you do not know His Word, then you cannot understand anything God wants you to do. If you do not get into the Word, it will totally stop your faith from working. You will be a person who is totally immobilized, or neutralized, in his or her faith. Nothing you try to do will ever prosper because there is no substance or background for it. Your faith will fail to produce.

Faith will not work unless you use it properly. You have to put a car in gear to drive it. You cannot sit back and say, "Faith, take over." You have to work it.

If you buy an exercise machine, you cannot sit on it all day long and expect to lose weight. You have to use the machine properly. It does take some understanding and effort on your part.

So, let faith start doing something *in* you and it will start doing something *for* you. As Christians, it is not that our faith is not working; it is simply a matter of not using it as God designed.

Paul wrote:

"There I also, after I heard of your faith in the Lord Jesus and your love for all the saints, do not cease to give thanks for you, making mention of you in my prayers: that the God of our Lord Jesus Christ, the Father of glory, may give to you the spirit of wisdom and revelation in the knowledge of Him, the eyes of your understanding being enlightened; that you may know what is the hope of His calling, what are the riches of the glory of His inheritance in the saints, and what is the exceeding

greatness of His power toward us who believe,
according to the working of His mighty power...."
(Ephesians 1:15-19)

It is possible that we lack certain knowledge
because we limit the ways in which we can learn. We
know some things by the perception and observation of
our five senses – and we know other things by
experiencing them. Paul gives us another way: with the
eyes of the heart. It takes a Spirit-filled believer to see
with the eyes of the heart, but that believer can see
things unbelievers cannot even imagine, much less
know.

When you have this kind of power going for you,
there will be no doubt in your heart about the blessing
God has for you. This I know, brothers and sisters;
only the eyes of the heart truly perceive Christian
knowledge. When the light-like presence of God
illuminates your heart, you will receive three gracious
gifts of Christian knowledge.

You will have the *spirit of wisdom*, wherein God
creates in you a new capacity for perception and
discernment. You will also experience the *spirit of
revelation*, the unexpected unveiling of divine truth that
takes place in the Gospel. And you will experience the
spirit of knowledge, full, deep, real, and participatory,
not a superficial acquaintance with God.

As you wait patiently in line for your order (or
blessing), you have high hopes – and such hope is
justified. However, just remember that the Object of
Christian hope (Jesus) is visible only to the eyes of the

heart. Christian hope is never merely within us; it lies before us.

Paul also wrote:

> "...*because of the hope which is laid up for you in Heaven, of which you have heard before in the word of the truth of the Gospel*...." (Colossians 1:5)

The great Object of our hope never varies. He is always before us. But, only the eyes of the heart can fasten on this hope. That is why, in order to see God's blessing for you, it is important to focus with eyes of the heart.

Here is something to think about: the church, as God's inheritance, is visible only to the eyes of the heart. Unbelievers only see the church as another organization, building, or institution, but the eyes of the heart see the church as God's inheritance, His estate, and His heritage. The darkened intellect, no matter what the person's IQ, cannot see God's plan for the ages worked out in the redemption of sinners who reflect the Lord's glory.

It is also only the eyes of the heart that can comprehend God's power. Paul exhausts every word in the Greek language to describe the power demonstrated in the Gospel. This massive accumulation of power is available to Christians in "*exceeding greatness.*"

That is why you do not have to worry about your order. God has the power to deliver it to you. Individual Christians and the church collectively may seem weak and ineffective, but when the Holy Spirit opens the eyes of the heart there is more power available to you than can be generated by every power company in the world, nuclear and otherwise.

But, there is this admonition from Jesus Christ:

"Except a man be born again he cannot see...." (John 3:3)

Lack of Love for Others

"For in Jesus Christ neither circumcision nor uncircumcision avails anything, but faith working through love." (Galatians 5:6)

When you do not operate in love, your faith will fail to produce. Everything you receive from God must be received through faith, and faith works by love. When you stop loving, your faith shuts down.

Love "employs" your faith.

Paul had a lot to say about love. For example:

"For this reason I bow my knees to the Father of the Lord Jesus Christ, from whom the whole family in Heaven and earth is named, that He would grant you, according to the riches of His glory, to be strengthened with might through His spirit in the inner man, that Christ may dwell in your hearts through faith; that you, being rooted and grounded in love, may be able to comprehend with all the saints what is the width and length and depth and height – to know the love of Christ which passes knowledge; that you may be filled with all the fullness of God." (Ephesians 3:14-19)

This prayer by Paul is one of the most fervent, comprehensive, and sublime in the Bible. It asks God for inner strength to comprehend His love and to experience His fullness. When you ask for and get that, you are going to have a blessing that makes everything else look small and insignificant.

I cannot stress this enough: the *power* necessary to love begins through prayer. This is a new power for your inner person. More than anything else in life, we need an infusion of the power, might, strength, and force of God. There is an inherent strength and dynamic energy in God's power that we desperately need – and the *place* in which we need that inner power is the "inner person." The "inner person" is the whole, conscious, person being. It is that secret spring of action that is within all of us.

And, we must experience that renewal daily. Paul writes:

> "*Therefore we do not lose heart. Even though our outward man is perishing, yet the inward man is being renewed day by day.*" (2 Corinthians 4:16)

Paul also addresses why we must have that inner renewal daily. It is because we are in a war between our inner being and the members of our body.

> "*For I delight in the law of God according to the inward man.*" (Romans 7:22)

When you ask something of God, you should not ask timidly – as if you are going to strain His resources.

You cannot ask too much of Him. The *proportion* by which God gives strength is nothing less than His *"riches in glory."* God does not give in proportion to our capacity or need, but His own perfection. Thus, the *person* of Christ is *at home* in our heart, a truly reigning presence – and is not merely a guest.

So strength to love *begins* with new power in the inner person.

There is, of course, a *necessary preparation* before we can understand Christ's love for us. We have to be "rooted and grounded" in our love for Him. And, if you are incapable of loving God after all that He has done for you – then you are incapable of truly loving anyone.

Anyway, we have to be rooted like a tree in the soil of Christian love, and founded like a building on the firm ground of love.

Only love understands love.

If you do not love Christ, you cannot understand His love for you. And, here is something else to put in your memory bank: if you fail to fellowship with God's people, you cannot grasp Christ's love. There must be *joint participation* "with all the saints" of Christ in order to understand God's love for us.

There is also an *external exploration* of Christ's love for us. When it comes to Jesus' love for us, we will spend forever seeking to know the unknowable and trying to measure the immeasurable – the extent of its breadth, the eternal duration of its length, the divinity of its height, and the humanity of its depth.

So, strength to love grows with a new comprehension of Christ's love for us.

Peter wrote:

> "...*by which have been given to us exceedingly great and precious promises, that through these you may be partakers of the divine nature, having escaped the corruption that is in the world through lust.*" (2 Peter 1:4)

For eternity we are to be *filled* with the totality of God's riches that can be given to the believer. Forever we are to receive until the limit of our capacity has been reached.

So strength of love finally *fills* the believer with the fullness of God.

Where there is *no love*, there is *no faith*. When you get out of the love walk, your faith shuts down. When you get into strife, you open the door to letting Satan abort your order.

Even the most mature Christian has to be aware of this pitfall of the enemy. We have to realize that placing an order with God is like carrying a pregnancy to full term. There are key phases of growth in each stage of development. You must develop in the area of love in order to be in a posture to receive from God.

Now that we have cleared that corner of life, we are approaching the first window. It is time to pay.

Chapter Four
TIME TO PAY
(The Difficult Part of Life)

We love to look at the menu. We love to place our order and sometimes we do not even mind turning the corner once we realize what we really want. The difficult part of life is when it is time to pay.

Everybody likes to place an order, and everybody likes to eat. Yet, the true hesitation comes when you have to reach into your pocket to give something in exchange for what you want. That hurts. The pain can vary based on how deep into your pocket you have to reach.

In life everybody has to pay in one form or another:

♦ Students have to pay by attending school for twelve years to get a high school diploma.

- ◆ You may have to make a down payment to move into your new home.

- ◆ You may have to put money down before you can buy your new car.

- ◆ You may have to take a series of shots before you can visit a foreign country.

For some of us, the cost may be higher because our orders may be greater or more detailed. Nevertheless, we will all pay.

In our Christian walk we go through personal persecutions and sufferings before we walk in peace. Losing people who are close to you can be costly, namely those who tell you, "I will never leave you." Then they notice how strong your walk with Christ has become and they let you know that they cannot relate to your new lifestyle.

At first there may be a temptation to go back to your old lifestyle. It may seem as if there is more benefit to living a life in the world than there is to being a Christian. But, after a while you will be able to move on. This is one of the prices you have to pay as a Christian: separation. Not everyone is going to want to be around you when you set a higher standard of living for yourself.

If we are going to be truly committed in our walk with the Lord, we are going to be attacked. The Bible says in Isaiah 54:17:

"No weapon formed against you shall prosper."

It does not say that the attack will not come. The Word of God promises that the weapons will not prosper. You will have the final victory.

The real strength of a tea bag is tested only when it is placed in hot water, and you will never know the real strength of your character until it has been tested by trials.

In life you will experience many difficulties, and you will be called on to make many sacrifices. You have to realize that whatever you want in life, you have to pay for it. So you must focus on your destination and not on your situation.

God wants you to know that there are several ways to get through the storms of life. There is no such thing as a storm-free existence. And, the major difference between a believer and a nonbeliever is the way he or she handles the storms of life. If you have a spiritual compass (the Bible), it tells you how to get through the storms of life. We should never look like what we are going through. It is important to know that anything worth having is worth paying for first.

Finally, you arrive at the window and are waiting to receive your order, but instead of immediately getting what you ordered, the person at the window repeats your order and says, "That will be five dollars and ninety-five cents."

You pay, but you still do not get your food. The person who took your money says, "Pull up to the next window, please."

It is time to move again and all you have for your money is a paper receipt. Of course, that paper receipt is all you need to lay claim to what you have just paid for. Your paper receipt is your claim ticket. It is proof that you have paid the price and, no matter how long it takes, you are entitled to get what you paid for.

The Bible is your receipt for the many blessings God has promised you. It is your claim ticket. It is the only proof you have that you are entitled to the blessings of God.

In the spiritual realm, faith is how we secure the blessings of God. But, what is faith and how do we get it? Paul tells us in the following Scripture:

> *"For I say, through the grace given unto me to every man that is among you, not to think of himself more highly than he ought to think; but to think soberly, according as God hath dealt to every man the measure of faith."* (Romans 12:3)

Faith is a *gift* from God.

So what is a *gift*?

It is something you *receive*.

You cannot buy a gift because if you pay for it, it is not a gift. So you do not have to do anything to get faith – just receive it.

Some people do not believe in healing. They do not believe because healing has not been taught in their church. You cannot have faith in something that you have not been taught.

People believe in salvation because salvation is taught in most evangelical churches on a regular basis.

They believe in baptism because it is taught and practiced on a regular basis in their church.

They believe in communion because communion is taught and practiced on a regular basis in their church.

But many people do not believe in God's miracles because those miracles are not being taught in many churches. When there is the experience of healing, speaking in tongues, and the working of other miracles in the lives of people, those who do not believe want to hush them up. If it is not preached or taught, believers do not have faith in these things. Very few people go to church looking for a *born again* experience. They go to church wanting a *feel good* experience that costs them absolutely nothing in terms of commitment.

Faith is a supernatural seed, but you can cause it to fail to produce. If you plant a watermelon seed in the carpet, it will not produce a watermelon. The seed is good, but the watermelon will not grow because somewhere between the seed and the planting there is no fertile soil where it can develop and grow.

So the seed (faith) does not always determine the outcome. Your actions, or reactions, can stop the productivity of the seed. You, as a Christian, have a lot to do with that seed. You have a lot to do with that faith being nurtured.

Some people say, "I'm a Christian and I have faith," but they take the supernatural seed that God provides and it never produces anything because they are not fertile ground in which something can grow.

The measure of faith God makes available to us is potent and strong. It is able to move mountains. Nothing is impossible for you when you truly trust God.

It is at the mountain where you really get to know your level of faith. If it were not for some of the mountains we encounter, some of us would never focus on where we need to be spiritually.

We would never grow.

Therefore, if you keep the faith, no matter how long it takes, you are going to get there. If you do not keep the faith and do not seek God, then your hope and your inspiration will die.

Do not get out of line and walk away from the blessings God has promised you. You can have the joy, everlasting peace, love, and all of those things Christ has to offer if you operate by faith and stay in line.

Paul wrote:

"So then faith cometh by hearing, and hearing by the word of God." (Romans 10:17)

Faith comes by hearing and hearing by the Word of God. If the Word is not preached, faith will not come. If faith does not come, you cannot believe. If you cannot believe, you cannot get faith. If you cannot get faith, you die and go to hell.

So, the gospel must be preached so that faith can come. Those who hear and receive will move from spiritual death to spiritual life. If the gospel is preached, sinners will be transformed and believers will be strengthened.

Before I became pastor of my church, I was a choir director. I was, more or less, a pastor to my choir. We had a choir (the Dallas Inspirational Choir) for about ten years, and I had been preaching for many years before I organized the choir.

During the first five years, we never experienced a manifestation of the gift of the Holy Spirit. We were all beautiful young people on fire for God, but there was not one divine healing or miracle. No person was filled with the Holy Spirit or spoke in tongues. For that first five years, however, on a regular basis many people were saved at every revival.

Do you know why?

It was because I only preached "salvation messages," so the faith in the congregations was only for salvation. They only believed God for saving them because that was all I preached.

If you do not hear anything else, you will not know anything else. If you do not know anything else, you cannot have faith for anything else.

You may say, "I've been praying and praying for faith, and I do not have any yet." You can pray until you are blue in the face, but you cannot pray for faith and you cannot fast for faith.

You may say, "Well, Pastor, I'm going to fast until my faith comes." You will never get faith by fasting. Faith does not come by praying or fasting.

If you are a believer, if you have been born again, you already have faith. "Born again" means you have accepted Jesus Christ as your personal Savior, you believe in Him, and you are living for Him. As a result of being born again, God gave you a measure of faith. You already have it.

The New Testament tells us:

"Now faith is the substance of things hoped for, the evidence of things not seen." (Hebrews 11:1)

Every Christian knows that Scripture by heart and can recite it at the drop of a hat. But, ask the same Christian to explain what it means and his or her reply is not given as quickly.

You cannot apply a definition to your circumstances and get results. You have to determine what the definition actually means and apply the meaning to your circumstances.

Many Christians live defeated lives because they only know what the Scripture *says* and not what the Scripture actually *means*. You cannot contract an illness, or a disease, and then say, *"Now faith is the substance of things hoped for, the evidence of things not seen."* It will not do you any good. You are correct in wanting to quote the Scripture, but quoting it will not change your circumstances. You must know what it means.

You might see friends and relatives receiving their desires without much time and effort. They might be getting houses, cars, spouses, better jobs, and a host of other things. Maybe you are still waiting to complete college, and maybe you are still single because God is making you into a companion equipped to have someone in your life who will not take your focus off Him.

But the important thing is that you are waiting. You are committed.

While I was still teaching high school theatre arts, evangelizing, traveling around the city, and directing the Dallas Inspirational Choir, I had several friends who were called to preach, who became pastors of large churches, and who really prospered in their ministries. During that time, I questioned God about my readiness to lead as a pastor, but honestly knew I was not ready.

Unfortunately, several of those friends who launched out before they were ready are no longer pastors – and some have even left their ministries.

I am glad I did not step out on my own, but instead waited for God to teach me how to be a compassionate leader. He enlarged my heart so I could genuinely love and be a good shepherd to His people. I am also thankful to God for giving me a servant leadership mentality. I am convinced that it was God who prepared me to lead a congregation and that it was not of my own doing. I had to decrease to allow God's anointing to increase my leadership abilities. He prepared me to be able to take the bites and nibbles of the sheep in my pasture.

Just as Jesus became flesh to live among people and to feel what they felt, I have that heart of humility as well. I was born poor. I know what it feels like to be hungry, to be evicted from your home. I am around people I can relate to. I thank God for not shielding me from hard times. Like Jesus, I walked in the shoes of hatred, lies, jealousy, and betrayal from my enemies, friends, and family. I never complained or gave up. I constantly continued to remember God's promises.

Here are a couple of questions you can ponder: Have you ever known a public figure to keep all his or her promises? Have you ever known God not to keep all His promises?

Once, after feeling emotionally weakened following a surprise attack from people whom I thought supported me, I announced to my congregation that I did not want anyone else to tell me they loved me. My feeling was that if love equated to persecution and betrayal, I would rather live without hearing those words.

Now, literally I did not mean that I did not ever want to hear those three words again. I just wanted people to *show* me that they loved me, and not just easily throw out any more empty expressions of love.

But, when I realized how quickly Satan had moved into my heart and discouraged me, I regretted speaking those words. You see, I had paid for that ridicule. I had committed my life to God's leadership, but those difficulties caused a temporary setback. Now I use my enemies as my footstool.

Paul said it much more eloquently than I can:

"I am crucified with Christ, nevertheless I live, yet not I, but Christ lives in me, and the life which I now live by the faith of the Son of God, who loves me, and gave Himself for me." (Galatians 2:20)

And, we should never forget Jesus' words:

"For God so loved the world that He gave His only begotten Son, that whosoever believeth in Him should not perish, but have everlasting life." (John 3:16)

I now wait on God to direct my life.

You have to wait as well.

Waiting builds character. It is not so important *that* we wait, but what is important is *how* we wait. It is what you do while you are waiting that makes a difference.

Are you complaining, mistreating others, or whining while waiting?

I hope not. What you should be doing is praying, meditating, and praising your way through any difficulties. When there is a decision that you cannot make, set the issue before God and wait on His answer.

We should not get so disrespectful that we do not care about complaining to God. God heard the complaints of the Israelites and He also hears ours.

Complaining is talking about something that you cannot change, and complaining about adversity is the worst complaining you can do. We tend to complain about our lives when people are trying to be like us – and vice versa.

God has entrusted a measure of adversity to all of us. It is not like that which anyone else suffers; it is all our own. But, He gives all of us grace to get through our adversity.

Everyone has something in his or her life that God does not want to hear him or her complain about. It is hard to live with adversity and not complain. But, we forfeit our grace that could help us get through our adversity by complaining about it.

We need to stop clinging to the idea of a perfect life on earth. If we had a perfect life here on earth, then we would have no reason to go to Heaven. God promised us that we would have tribulations, and that He would deliver us out of them all. The adversity we complain about is the thing that keeps us close to Him. Our complaining is what puts us in the wilderness. God will not tolerate repeated complaints.

The psalmist wrote:

"Many are the afflictions of the righteous; but the Lord delivers him out of them all." (Psalm 34:19)

When you establish a good prayer life, you cultivate cues, or gentle prompts, from God. While you are waiting on God, the Holy Spirit will prompt you to pray. Anything that has value will cost you something, and in this case it is patience. Your effort to wait sets God in motion. It takes a mature person to show patience. When you are patient, God is pleased with your maturity, and God will strengthen you while you are waiting.

One day as I was studying the Word of God, I received the revelation that faith is the key that operates everything in the Spirit realm. In order to receive anything from God, we *must* operate by faith. Then I learned that in order to effectively use my faith, I had to realize the *time* of faith.

You see, there is a time when faith is faith, and there is a time when faith is not faith. In order to have a successful life, it is important to know the difference between the two.

I am sure you have heard people say, "Well, I know the Lord will make a way." When you say this, you mean it from the bottom of your heart, but it is not a true statement. Saying you know God *will* do something will never bring you the desired manifestation of God's promises. It sounds good – and even sounds like faith – but it is really just the opposite.

The most important thing you can learn about faith is that it has a time. In other words, when is faith really faith?

If you are waiting right now, ask yourself, "Am I really waiting in faith, or am I waiting because I have to? Am I content with God's timing, or do I feel it is taking Him too long?"

The Scripture says, *"Now faith is...."*

Because faith is present tense, faith is always *now*. If it is not now, then it is not faith. In other words, when you say, "God is going to do....," you are saying He has *not* done it yet. "Going to" implies the action will take place in the future. God is not a future tense

God and will never move on behalf of a future tense confession. God is present tense and faith is always *now*. If it is not *now*, it is not faith. When you operate in faith, God wants you to know that it is already done. That is why the things that God has promised you are already yours.

If you say God is *going* to do something, you deny that He has already done it. Therefore, your confession is working against your faith. People do not properly operate by faith because they are looking at the future and do not understand that God has already done what He said He would do.

Just because you do not have your order in your hand right now does not mean you do not have it. It only means you cannot see it. So, when you place your order and you are instructed to move forward, you have the strength to stay in line because you know that it is already done. If you stay in line thinking God is *going* to answer, you might as well get out of line because you will never receive anything.

Because we do not understand the timing of faith, and that God has already answered our prayers, we give up on God and bless ourselves. We find our own spouses. We find our own jobs. We find our own houses. And, because these things were not obtained with God's help, we end up with a disaster on our hands.

While your order is being prepared, God is preparing you for your order. Sometimes the problem is not what you ask for, but the condition you are in when you ask. Remember: as long as God is, faith is.

The second part of that Scripture says, *"The substance of things hoped for..."*

Again, we need to translate this into a meaning we can apply to our situation. This Scripture is personal. It speaks to us where we are, not where we are going to be, or where we have been.

So, what is substance?

Substance is tangible, meaning you can experience it with your senses. So we can interpret the Scripture this way: *Now, faith is that thing for which you are hoping, which you can touch, taste, smell, hear, or see.*

Hope must be accompanied by faith in order for it to be effective. Hope alone has no substance. There is nothing about hope that you can *touch, taste, smell, hear, or see* because if you could, then you would not need any faith.

Faith must be very important in order for it to be the substance for things that are hoped for. When we add faith to our hope, then we give our hope substance. Hope sets the goal, but faith goes and gets it.

You must, obviously, have hope. You cannot live without it. But, if you do not have some way to reach your hope, then your hope will never have anything that you can ever *touch, taste, smell, hear, or see.*

Now you understand why the devil wants to destroy your hope. If you have no hope, you have nothing to have faith for or in. No matter what happens, never lose hope.

Financially, you may have a pretty hard struggle, but hope will keep you afloat. Hope, however, does not bring you out of your financial problem; it just keeps you alive until you get out.

Hope will let you smile while the ship is sinking, but faith will keep the ship afloat. You can smile while it is going down, or you can believe and keep it floating.

Hope affects your attitude about the circumstances, but faith will change the circumstances. Hope makes you handle what you are going through like you are not going through it, but faith will change it. Faith is working underneath the circumstances, while hope makes it look like it is already done.

Faith digs a tunnel to your blessing. Hope makes it appear as if it is already finished. That is the difference in hope and faith.

It is not easy at this point because you still do not have what you have asked for. Usually at this point you begin to wonder, "God, is there something wrong? Why is nothing happening?"

Do you feel stuck even though you know you are operating in a degree of faith? Well, what you are experiencing now is simply a temporary delay. What you must do is commit to the delay and wait until God moves. During the delay, the devil will take every opportunity to try and make you get out of line. Just remember that a delay is not a denial. It only means God is working some things out. A delay is your friend, because during a delay God is not only preparing you for your blessing, He is also preparing your blessing for you. During the delay, make preparations to possess the promises of God.

God knows and sees the end from the beginning. He does not get nervous about the future, nor does He stay up worrying and biting His nails all night. So, although things may not look good now, just keep diligently seeking Him by faith and you will be rewarded. Do not give up on your dream, or on all the good things that God has promised. Whatever you asked for in prayer, you have already received it in the Spirit – and if you can just hold on to your faith and be patient, no matter what happens in the interim, you will receive it in due season. No matter how you feel, do not give up.

God tells us that it is important to win over worry. Jesus put it very succinctly when He said:

> *"Therefore I say to you, do not worry about your life, what you will eat or what you will drink; nor about your body, what you will put on. Is not life more than food and the body more than clothing? Look at the birds of the air, for they neither sow nor reap nor gather into barns; yet your heavenly Father feeds them. Are you not of more value than they? Which of you by worrying can add one cubit to his stature? So why do you worry about clothing? Consider the lilies of the field, how they grow: they neither toil nor spin; and yet I say to you that even Solomon in all his glory was not arrayed like one of these. Now if God so clothes the grass of the field, which today is, and tomorrow is thrown into the oven, will He not much more clothe you, O you of little faith? Therefore do*

not worry, saying, 'What shall we eat? Or 'What shall we drink?' or 'What shall we wear?' For after all these things the Gentiles seek. For your heavenly Father knows that you need all these things. But seek first the kingdom of God and His righteousness, and all these things shall be added to you. Therefore do not worry about tomorrow, for tomorrow will worry about its own things. Sufficient for the day is its own trouble." (Matthew 6:25-34)

Worry has never been a part of God's plan for you. Worry stems from a lack of trust in God, which is revealed in the way we react when we are under pressure. If you are a worrier, you need to be careful. Did you know that you could worry yourself right into a hospital bed? Worrying suppresses the body's immune system and prevents the release of hormones that your body needs to stay healthy. We must trust God enough to avoid worry and be mature enough to embrace faith so that His Holy Spirit can flow through us and give us comfort when we are going through difficult times.

I am not saying that bad things do not happen. We have already established that they do. I am saying that if Satan can get you to react by worrying when bad things do happen, he can take advantage of the opportunity to make you miserable. So put all your worries to sleep and awaken your faith. When you make up your mind that you are going to trust God with all of your heart, you make a decision not to worry.

One of your greatest victories in life could be winning over worry. You can stop worrying about life's lower anxieties – food, drink, and clothing – when you give yourself to life's greatest concern, the kingdom of God.

If you want to be truly blessed, stop worrying about the secular. Heed Jesus' command and do not become distracted with the basics of life. God's greatest gifts always include the lesser. Worry is unnecessary, unavailing, and unbecoming.

It is also important to stop worrying about future uncertainty. You can master the demons of worry if you confine them to today. Worrying about what is going to happen, which is almost always tomorrow, does absolutely no good.

You can stop worrying by substituting the great concern above all others. That great concern is verse thirty-three of the aforementioned scripture:

"But seek first the kingdom of God and His righteousness..."

This is a command, not an option. It is a habit, a continual way of life for a Christian. And, you will not be focusing on lesser concerns if your eyes are on the greater concern.

Faith is Acting on the Word of God

Sometimes the Word of God instructs us to do things that seem ridiculous. Someone steals your purse, and the Word of God instructs you to pray for him or her. That may seem impossible, but if God says to do it, do it.

We tend to look at situations in the natural way and say they are impossible because of what our five senses tell us, but with God all things are possible. God may ask you to do something that seems impossible to you because you have never done it before. You may even ask, "How can I do that? How can I love somebody who persecutes me and talks about me?"

It is possible because Jesus commands us to love our enemies and to pray for them. I know it seems like an unachievable task, but it is a command, not an option.

At Thy Word

When it came to worrying and fretting about some of the things in life, Peter was in a league all his own. He was always questioning, worrying, and then getting a dose of reality from Christ that caused him to lament his doubt. For example:

> *"Now when He had stopped speaking, He said to Simon, 'Launch out into the deep and let down your nets for a catch.' But Simon answered and said to Him, 'Master, we have toiled all night and caught nothing; nevertheless at Your Word I will let down the net.' And when they had done this, they caught a great number of fish, and their net was breaking. So they signaled to their partners in the other boat to come and help them. And they came and filled both the boats, so that they began to sink. When Simon Peter saw it, he fell down at Jesus' knees, saying, 'Depart from me, for I am a sinful man, O Lord!' For he and all who were with him were astonished at the catch of fish which they had*

taken; and so also were James and John, the sons of Zebedee, who were partners with Simon. And Jesus said to Simon, 'Do not be afraid. From now on you will catch men.' So when they had brought their boats to land, they forsook all and followed Him." (Luke 5:4-11)

You may ask, "What does God know about my problems? God has never had a nagging husband." Now, you brothers can substitute "nagging wife" for "nagging husband." Neither gender has a monopoly on *nagging.*

Or, you might say, "God has never had a runaway teenager. God does not have any problems. What does God know about high blood pressure? God's never been sick, so what does God know about what I'm going through?"

Peter could have had the same attitude. He had been fishing all night and had caught nothing. But, Jesus told him to go back one more time and let down his net.

Can you not just imagine Peter, cutting his eyes back at the other disciples and getting an attitude with Jesus?

So Jesus told Peter to go out into the deep. Just imagine what Peter was thinking. "Now, why would He send me back out here? Doesn't He realize we have already done this all night and there were no fish to be caught?"

Peter did not realize that this time would be different. Jesus had changed the circumstances. He had made the fish gather before He sent Peter back to cast his nets again.

Have you ever waited for something so long that it seemed easier to just give up hope of ever receiving it? Peter had toiled all night, but at Jesus' request, Peter said, "Nevertheless, at Thy Word, I will let down the net."

Peter's act of obedience to Jesus' request provided him with so many fish that the boat almost sank from the weight of the load.

That is the secret to faith: "*At Thy Word…*"

Peter acted on what Jesus told him to do and received a boatload of fish. When the only thing you have is God's Word, God's Word is all you need. Perhaps you need a job right now. You have to say, "Father, I am going on this interview. I do not qualify. I do not have a college degree, but, nevertheless, at Thy Word." If you never act on it, you will never receive it.

Many things that are written in the Bible may seem impossible. But are they? Peter said, "*We have toiled all night and we have taken nothing.*" It is one thing to work and get some sign of change, but to work all night and have nothing to show for it is quite another.

Here is a situation that seemed absolutely impossible. These men were experienced fishermen, but it seemed that on this day nothing would come from their efforts. They did this work every day and night of their lives. It was their job.

These men knew the sea. They knew about schools of fish, where to look for fish, and how to read the tide and the wind. They had toiled all night long. Then along comes Jesus, a carpenter's son, who knows nothing about fishing, and He says to Peter, "*Let down your nets for a draught.*"

I am sure Peter was thinking that what was being asked of him was totally ridiculous. "*We have toiled all night, and we have taken nothing; but, nevertheless, at Thy Word, I'll let down the net.*"

And, the Bible says when they had done this they enclosed a great multitude of fishes.

Faith and Belief

Perhaps you are a new believer, one who is going to take God at His Word. You are not just going to take note of God's Word and believe it, but you are going to activate that belief. Maybe you are strong in the faith, but there is something that you need to understand about what is going on in your life right now and why you are not receiving what you want from God.

There are two words throughout the Scriptures that are used separately and independently, but in the natural, we tend to make these same words synonymous. Those words are *faith* and *belief.*

Most people think faith and belief are the same. They think believing is faith – and that faith is belief. You may think, "I believe, then that is faith and if I have faith, then that means that I believe."

I thought that myself for a long time. As a matter of fact, I even preached about it. I thought that to believe was to have faith and to have faith was to believe. When I did not see any changes, I began to seek God for an answer as to why my prayers were going unanswered.

That is why, in my life, I was defeated and wondered why other Christians received their blessings and I did not. I had the same belief. I believed just like they believed. I had faith just like they had faith. I knew my name was written in the Lamb's Book of Life and that had I dropped dead at any point in my life, I knew without a doubt that I would have gone to Heaven. But, in terms of everyday living, I did not have any victory in my life and I had no evidence of my prayers being answered.

You may be the same way. You know that if you were to die right now you would go to Heaven, but right now things are just not working in your favor. You may be like I was. I was frustrated, in debt, and fearful about the future. I did not know what was going to happen tomorrow and I worried all the time about whether things were going to work out in my favor.

Of course, I prayed and went through all the motions of prayer, but with no results. In terms of praying and receiving specific things that I desired, I did not get a response. I thought that because I believed God's Word I was exercising faith, but I was not. I eventually learned something that would change my prayer life: I learned the difference between faith and belief.

Faith and belief are two sides of the same coin. Take a coin out of your pocket and look at it. When you look at the coin, you will notice that one side has someone's face on it and the other side has an eagle or a building. Every coin has two sides. It is one coin and it is only good with both sides – a head side and a tail side. To spend the coin, you need both sides intact. One side will not do you any good.

Faith and belief are the same way. Faith is the acceptance of the Word of God, while belief is having confidence in the Word of God. They are only effective together. If you do not know the difference between faith and belief, you will never be able to exercise your faith.

Here is Scripture that really speaks to what I am talking about:

> *"But be ye doers of the Word, and not hearers only, deceiving your own selves. For if any be a hearer of the Word, and not a doer, he is like unto a man beholding his natural face in a glass...."* (James 1:22:23)

You must speak your words from your lips when you pray, not think them in your mind. You must verbalize those desires so that God will hear them. You did not pull up to the menu board and think your order. You spoke your order so it could be heard. You have to speak those desires into existence. He will answer your prayers because you believe that He will. You must put your faith first before you receive. Knowing that you will receive is putting faith in action.

Several years ago I taught a faith lesson and used an illustration where a starving man was told that unless he ate the food in his hand, he would die of starvation. The man had ten minutes to live, and unless he ate the food he would die of starvation.

With food in hand, the man recited, "I believe that if I eat this food, I will not die of starvation."

Time ticks away until he has only ten seconds remaining, but instead of eating the food and living, the man continues to say, "I believe that if I eat this food, I will not die of starvation."

Countdown begins: ten, nine, eight, seven, six, five, four, three, two, one, zero.

The man dies.

He not only had to have faith that eating the food would save his life, he had to act on his faith (exercise his faith) and decide to eat the food.

Some people read the Bible once and figure, "Well, I know what the Bible says about that."

That is not the way to allow faith to come. Reading the Bible once or twice is not enough to provoke spiritual maturity. You cannot just read it once or twice and figure you know what the Bible says about a particular situation.

Some Christians read the Bible as if it was a newspaper or a magazine, but the Bible is the Living Word. It is a living organism. It is not just about *reading,* it is about *doing.* If you do not *do* it, then you do not *know* it. No matter how much you talk about how you believe the Bible, if you do not act on what the Bible says, it is not going to do you any good in your everyday life.

The second part of the verse says, *"He is like unto a man beholding his natural face in a glass..."* The Word of God is a mirror. To achieve God's desired results for you, hold that mirror up every day of your life. As you look in God's mirror, you see these truths: You are a born-again Christian, and you have faith that overcomes the world. You have been granted the authority to use the name of Jesus and walk in victory, but until you start doing something about what you believe, it is not faith. Faith must be accompanied by a corresponding action.

Here is how faith works: first, you are given information, you believe the information, and then you act on the information. On your job, what guarantee do you have that you are going to get paid on payday? None. You have no proof and you have no guarantee, but yet you work. You act on your employer's word. Do you trust in your employer's word more than you trust God's Word?

Whether we want to admit it or not, many Christians do.

Do you get paid every day? No. But, you work every day because you are acting on the word of a natural man or woman – your employer.

We should, obviously, give God more consideration and trust than we give our employer. Because we have God's written Word on it, we have His guarantee.

When you put action to your faith, wonderful things happen.

Everything I believe by faith, I act on. How do I act on it? I act on it by taking it to God. In every instance in the Bible when people believed God, they took their request to Him.

Take particular note of the following Scripture:

"And when they were come to the multitude, there came to him a certain man, kneeling down to him, and saying, 'Lord, have mercy on my son: for he is lunatic, and sorely vexed: for oftentimes he falls into the fire, and into the water. And I brought him to thy disciples, and they could not cure him.'" (Matthew 17:14-16)

In this Scripture we can see faith's corresponding action. The man believed the disciples could heal his son. So the man brought him. The action is in the fact that the man *brought* the child. Even though the disciples could not heal the man's son and he was actually healed by Jesus, he was still healed. If you believe something, act on what you believe – and when you do, begin to respond to the answer and not to the problem.

So here you are. You have placed your order, you have cleared the corner, you have paid the price, and now you are waiting on your order.

Most people do not receive what they ask God for because they do not really want to wait. The real problem is holding onto faith while waiting. It is during your wait when you encounter most of your conflict with the enemy. This is called frustration.

Chapter Five
WHAT'S THIS WAIT ABOUT?
(The Frustrating Part of Life)

Congratulations! You have accomplished an enormous part of your wait in line, considering that you are trusting in someone you cannot see. It is obvious that you have come too far, and invested too much, to get out of line now.

You are probably beginning to realize just how long you have been in line. This is definitely the time when Satan will do everything he can to discourage you in the hope that you will try to run on ahead of God. You have to constantly think about the reason you are waiting. You are waiting because God – the Head Cook, who knows all -- is preparing your order. He is performing a divine work in you while you are on your journey.

Think about it: while in a drive-through, you prepare yourself to receive your order by cleaning out your cup holder or rearranging items in your car.

Well, that is exactly what God wants to do while you are waiting. He wants to cleanse your heart from past hurts and teach you to forgive, clearing the way for you to be in a receiving position.

The question is not if you are going to wait, because we know waiting is a part of our lives. The real question has to do with what you choose to do while waiting. To keep yourself in position to receive, you can:

Meditate on God's Word

- ♦ Meditate on God's Word

- ♦ Use Your Imagination Positively

- ♦ Expect to be Blessed

- ♦ Understand the Enemy's Aim

As you are waiting for your order to be filled, you need to start believing God. You can start by developing a stronger relationship with God, which will result in trusting Him to do what He says He will do. Trust comes as you learn more about God and His promises. And, by reading God's Word daily, you can start occupying yourself with positive thoughts.

You also need to meditate on God's Word so that it will be absorbed deep down in your heart where it can make a difference. There are a lot of people affiliated with various religious cults who have perverted meditation and who are receiving perverted results. Please understand that I am not talking about this type of meditation. Meditation, simply stated, means to dwell on something in thought repeatedly. To begin to experience God's kind of success, you must get His Word down deep in your heart, which requires hearing and acting upon the Word (God's Word).

There is a Scripture in the Old Testament that is particularly appropriate here:

> *"This Book of the Law* (which is God's Word) *shall not depart out of thy mouth; but thou shall meditate therein day and night, that thou may observe to do according to all that is written therein: for then thou shall make thy way prosperous, and then thou shall have* (not just success) *good success."* (Joshua 1:8)

Meditation can play a major role in successfully transporting you from the problem to the answer. When you *read and memorize* the Word of God, it is placed in your mind so that you can recall it. By contrast, when you *meditate* on the Word of God, it is planted in your heart.

It is not until the Word is "planted" deeply that you can expect results. As you make it a habit to study and meditate on the Word of God, desires will be created in your heart. The Word is the tool God uses to create desires in your heart.

I am sure you can tell by now that I believe God's Word should be used in your daily life. Some people tend to use the Word of God like a first-aid kit, but that is an improper use. That is equivalent to learning CPR while somebody is having a heart attack. Oftentimes, people do not start praying until a crisis hits. But, when trials show up in our lives, we should already have the Word sown in our hearts so that it can act as a repellent against Satan's damaging effects.

A Challenge

I challenge you to try meditation for the next seven days.

I want you to locate one Bible verse or Scripture that you can apply to your wait in line. There is no doubt in my mind that this will change your whole spiritual life.

Spend fifteen to twenty minutes meditating on that Scripture. Just walk around and speak it while going about your day. Say it over and over. Make a song out of it.

When you lie down at night, say it while you are in bed. Your spirit will continue to soak it up while you sleep. When you wake up, read that Scripture again and start the process over. You will find that the truth will become more and more alive within you – and the Word of God will be planted deeper and deeper in your heart.

Many exercise experts have taught us that a small amount of physical exercise (twenty to thirty minutes a day) can give us the physical results we want. You must use this same concept when it comes to your spiritual life. Learning to flex your spiritual muscles by meditating on God's Word is just what you need. One major reward of meditation is that you are utilizing your mind's eye (your imagination) as an effective tool to get past this tough point in your waiting period.

Use Your Imagination Positively

Using your imagination God's way can get you healed and delivered. All you have to do is imagine yourself as God sees you, which is only according to His Word. For example:

If your order request from God is physical, just imagine yourself feeling better from your illness.

If it is financial, imagine yourself with money and, before long, it will come to pass.

Only when you do these things in God's way and in God's order, according to your faith, will your imagination effectively produce.

Think of the many times you have walked into a store, looked at a dress or a suit, and said, "I can see myself wearing that."

Think of the many times you have passed a car and mumbled, "I can see myself driving that." You can almost feel the steering wheel in your hands. You might be driving a dump now, but the truth is that your dream car is on the way.

You use your imagination to meditate on all sorts of things all the time, so why not use it as a tool to help you get through the waiting period? When you are meditating on the Word day and night, you are reminding yourself of God's actual words to you. This will ignite your faith and endurance so that you can wait, no matter how long it takes your blessing to manifest.

Intellectual study of the Word of God is not enough. Instead, you must create a habit of imagining your desires and then thinking on them daily. Desires, birthed as a result of meditation and imagination on God's Word, will proceed directly into the listening ear of God. Remembering that He hears you will make you a person of expectancy. Some of us act as if we do not think God is watching us while we are waiting, but that is untrue. He is watching and listening.

Expect to be Blessed

The Word of God leaves nothing to chance regarding your blessing, as the following Scripture promises:

"There is surely a future hope for you and your expectation will not be cut off." (Proverbs 23:18)

You must begin to seriously expect God to answer your prayers. Expectation means to anticipate or look for something to happen. Expectation colors your outlook and shapes your attitude because it influences your actions. Expectation not only involves a change of your vision and your faith, but also a change in your level of living.

When a woman is expecting a child, her expectation triggers a lot of preparation. Spiritually speaking, expectation implies preparation as well. So you had better get ready for what God is doing for you. It seems, I am sure, that you are just waiting on God, but the truth of the matter is that God is waiting on you. If you really expect God to do something in your life, you need to begin to prepare yourself and your surroundings.

A catcher in baseball must first get in the proper posture to receive the pitch he expects to be thrown at him – fastball, curveball, slider, or whatever. His posture gives a signal to the rest of the team that he is ready to receive the pitch. Many times, we are not in the proper position, or posture, to receive from God. It *is not always a matter of God not being ready to deliver, but that we are not ready to receive.*

Are you ready?

Ask yourself, "What is the condition of my heart?"

"Do I have the right attitude?"

"Can God trust me with a blessing?"

"How can I be a blessing to someone else?"

"Are my motives right?"

These and other questions like these will condition your heart and move you into the proper spiritual posture to receive.

As a child, I remember standing on the curb watching a parade go by, and all the kids around me received candy. I wondered, "Why are they giving all that candy to those kids?" Then I noticed that the kids were showing them that they wanted the candy by stretching out their hands.

Show God that you are ready to receive by stretching forth your hands in praise. We should be in the posture of praise while we are waiting on God to manifest our prayers. We should never be found questioning God about how much longer it is going to take, or checking on the holdup. We must trust our Heavenly Father enough to know that He knows exactly when to provide us with what we ask for.

When you get a little weary from waiting, praise anyhow. If you are in the midst of a trial, praise anyhow.

The psalmist wrote:

"My soul, wait thou only upon God; for my expectation is from Him." (Psalm 62:5)

A properly focused expectation says, "I am not looking for anyone else other than God to answer my prayer."

If you really want to receive anything from God, you must begin to cultivate your expectancy. Many people are not healed because they do not expect to be healed. Their level of expectancy is too low. If you want a healing, if you want a financial increase, if you want a miracle, you must raise your level of expectancy.

As a teenage boy, my body was afflicted with a crippling disease called Guillain-Barre Syndrome. As a result of this, I spent months in a coma, with family and

Pastor Rickie G. Rush
www.rickierush.com

friends all around me who could offer me no help. Upon finally awakening, I was told that my chances of walking again were very slim, and that there was also the fear of possible brain damage.

After enduring many months of physical therapy, being transported in wheelchairs, wearing leg braces, and walking with the assistance of crutches and canes, God restored the full use of my legs. To this day, there is no medical record of my being cured, but, thanks to God, I am better than cured – I am healed and whole.

What the medical doctors could not do, God did with one touch of His hand. Even now, there are times when the pain associated with this syndrome affects my body. I have suffered many attacks from the enemy as he tries to get me to give in to the pain of this affliction, but I refuse. By faith in Christ, I walk in divine health, confess my healing daily, and God delivers daily.

Honestly, in the natural, sometimes I get tired of saying, "I believe I'm healed." Then I quickly remember that I do not get tired of being healed. Each time I confess my healing, it promotes the manifestation of my heart's desire to be healed. I begin to feel better and I have to say it whether I feel like it or not.

Confession of God's Word, mixed with faith, will bring about manifestation every time. This is an infallible truth, and I am living proof. In I Peter 2:24, it is written, *"By His stripes I am healed."* And, as long as I have God's Word in me, I will experience healing.

By confessing divine healing in my body, I am able to carry out God's purpose for my life on a daily basis.

My responsibility is to confess the healing, and God's responsibility is to bring it to pass in my life. Always remember that our confession must be based on what God says in His Word.

Now, does that mean that you cannot have any thoughts of your own? No, of course not. You have a brain and He wants you to think, but you must allow your thinking to align with God's thinking. You can still put it in your own words, but it is coming from what God says you can have in His Word.

The key is finding a Scripture that supports your desire and holding onto it until the blessings have manifested in your life. Healing was my desire, so I found a Scripture to support my healing, and I confessed it until my healing was manifested. Wait on your order from God with expectancy.

The following Scripture is a great lesson for us:

"Now Peter and John went up together to the temple at the hour of prayer, the ninth hour. And a certain man lame from his mother's womb was carried, whom they laid daily at the gate of the temple which is called Beautiful, to ask alms from those that entered the temple; who, seeing Peter and John about to go into the temple, asked for alms. And fixing his eyes on him, with John, Peter said, 'Look on us.' So he gave them his attention, expecting to receive something from them. Then Peter said, 'Silver and gold I do not have, but what I do have I give you: In the name of Jesus Christ of Nazareth, rise up and walk.' And he took him by the right hand and lifted him up, and immediately

his feet and anklebones received strength. So he, leaping up, stood and walked and entered the temple with them – walking, leaping, and praising God. And all the people saw him walking and praising God. Then they knew that it was he who sat begging alms at the Beautiful Gate of the temple; and they were filled with wonder and amazement at that which had happened to him. Now as the lame man who was healed held on to Peter and John, all the people ran together to them in the porch which is called Solomon's, greatly wondering." (Acts 3:1-11)

Here is a man who always begged and had been crippled all his life. He probably never really expected to work, or walk, because he always begged.

Before I knew God the way I know God now, I was a person who always begged. I was so good at begging that all I had to do was look, and everyone around me knew I needed something!

This man kept his eyes on the ground in humility and shame as he begged from Peter and John. Peter, sensing the man needed a change in posture, commanded him to "*Look on us.*"

Peter demanded that the beggar change his posture, and because Peter's demand had an effect on the man, he looked up. When Peter said to him, "*Silver and gold have we none, but such as we have we give unto you,*" he was letting the man know that they had something that far exceeded his expectation. But, in order for him to receive it, he would have to first change his posture.

In other words, he needed to look up and then get up.

After Peter had spoken, he grabbed the man by his hand and pulled him to his feet. Suddenly this man's feet and ankles gained strength and be began to praise God.

What is God saying with this Biblical account?

He is saying that when you really expect something to happen, it changes everything.

Understand the Enemy's Aim

The devil's goal is to make you get out of line so that you never receive your blessings from God. You have to believe by faith that your order has been received, is being prepared, and will be delivered to you at the right time.

When we asked God for a new church and all the extras, we had to wait in line just like everybody else. We looked around and saw that everybody was building churches, everybody had congregations, and everybody owned property. By this time our church had become very crowded and we were up to four church services every Sunday – and we could see no sign that God was answering our prayer.

Having grown a little impatient with waiting, we decided it was taking God a little too long. We were tempted by Satan to get out of line and seek our own answers, especially after applying for loans at seven banks and being rejected by all seven. We then decided to take one million, nine hundred thousand dollars and invest in a company that promised to give us an excellent return on our investment, which we would use for the purchase of a new church. Unfortunately, we were deceived and lost the one million, nine hundred thousand dollars.

We were humiliated, thinking everybody was laughing and making fun of us for being deceived. When we came to our end, the Holy Spirit said to us, "Now that you have tried it your way, sit back and watch God work."

When I talked to God about the church we needed, I pulled up to the menu and placed my order according to the promises of God:

"Therefore I say to you, whatever things you ask when you pray, believe that you will receive them and you will have them." (Mark 11:24)

I said, "Lord, there are some things we want." The Lord had let me know that whatever things I desired for the church would be manifested. I said, "Lord, we need a larger church. We want an ice cream parlor, weight rooms, racquetball court, game room, theater, playstation rooms, video arcades, billiards room, gym, recreation center, and fitness track."

I even asked that God give us a cafeteria, a bridal parlor, and a bowling alley. Oh yeah, and a store.

By the way, once you get God on the line, keep Him until you get *all* your order in.

It is not surprising that God blessed us tremendously with millions of dollars to purchase the building we now own. He even went above and beyond what we asked for by blessing us to totally pay off the loan in two years.

God deserves all the glory.

What a valuable lesson we learned from what was an awful experience – trying to do it on our own. You do not have to see what God is doing to believe Him. If you are to believe Him, believe Him by faith and trust Him with all your heart.

The time you are most tempted to get out of line and quit is when you must remember not to be weary in well doing.

Why?

You are going to reap if you just get tough enough to wait. Do not get tired of acting, confessing, and living God's word. Do not get tired of standing for your healing. Do not get tired of giving – and do not get tired of loving.

Keep planting seeds in good ground. Your due season and your blessings are coming.

The Bible says we will receive if we do not faint (get tired of waiting and give up). Do not get out of line and stop believing God for your purpose. Where the promises of God are concerned, it is not a matter of "if" He is going to come through; it is a matter of "when" He is going to come through.

Only God knows how many times many of us have quit right before our due season arrived. What you have to understand is that the closer you get to receiving, the more pressure the devil applies. He wants you to get out of line.

Do you see now why it can take so long to get to your blessing? We want God's blessing, but when it does not come when and the way we want it to come, we tend to quit.

If you do not give up under the pressure of your circumstances and under the pressure of those who mock and laugh at you, then you will reap. Stick with it! What you must realize is that progress is being made in the spirit realm that you cannot see, and you will not be able to see it until it breaks through into the natural realm. God is working it out underneath the surface. A lot can be happening underneath the surface that you can never perceive or imagine. So, what you must understand is that when you cannot see any sign, God is still working it out.

The Scripture says:

"For consider Him who endured such hostility from sinners against himself, lest you become weary and discouraged (faint) in your souls." (Hebrews 12:3)

Where does the discouragement or fainting start? Fainting starts in the mind. The mind is where the battle of faith is won or lost. Satan's method is to whisper suggestions that you should think about giving up on God and going against God's plan for your life.

Unfortunately, one trick Satan uses very effectively against God's children is "self-talk." Self-talk is when you speak negatively to yourself and speak opposite of

God's Word. If the self-talk you engage in is negative, you probably say things like, "Maybe I am not worthy of God's blessings." Or, "Maybe God does not really want me to have this."

When these negative thoughts arise in your mind, you must dismiss them and replace them with God's Word. Do what Jesus did. When Satan's aim was to interfere with Jesus' mission here on earth, Jesus would always say, "*It is written...*"

Jesus' meaning was clear: whatever He was dealing with, something was written in the Holy Scriptures to handle it. He did not have to fight Satan with anybody's word but God's. Saying "*It is written...*" is like calling in the Heavenly police to remind Satan of the promises of God that are written in the Word. You are reminding him that his future has already been determined, and that you realize that he has no power over you. What is written in God's Word is the secret weapon we must use to continue to live in victory on earth.

Think on what is written here:

> "*For the vision is yet for an appointed time, but at the end it shall speak, and not lie: though it tarry, wait for it; because it will surely come, it will not tarry.*" (Habakkuk 2:3)

Many Christians are guilty of moving ahead of God and trying to answer their own prayers. Maybe God has given you a vision for ministry. Well, you must learn to wait on God's due season. One of the hardest things for a Christian to do while waiting on God's timing is to be patient when there is a burning desire in his or her heart.

If you believe God has promised you something, write it down, and do not let anybody else see it. But, sometimes you just cannot. What do I mean by "sometimes you just cannot"? Well, for example, have you ever had someone set you up with a date when they knew you desired a companion? Has a friend ever told you about a car when he knew you were looking for one?

Sometimes you just cannot tell anyone what you prayed for because they might try to answer your prayer for you. If you tell people your desires, they may try to fill them, thinking they are helping you. Only God knows how to fill your order. When you start feeling impatient or weary, remember that there is an appointed time for your blessing. Some things you have to keep between you and God until they are received. Everyone may not be able to receive your blessing, or understand why you are waiting on God to give you what you want.

In speaking to God – spending time with Him – the Holy Spirit laid something very heavy on me about moving before the time is right. Think about these questions:

- Can Satan trick you?

- Can Satan deceive you?

- Can you buy the wrong car?

- Can you buy it at the wrong time?

- Can you pay the wrong price for it?

- Can you buy the wrong house?

- Can you get it at the wrong time?

- Can you buy a house for the wrong reasons?

- Can you marry the wrong person?

- Can you marry at the wrong time?

- Can you marry for the wrong reason?

- Can you get involved with the wrong person at the wrong time for the wrong reasons?

- Is it possible for somebody else to have married your wife or husband before you ever met her or him?

The answer to all these questions is *yes*, when Satan gets involved.

Since Satan is a deceiver and he comes to steal, kill, and destroy, realize that most of his diabolical plans were placed in motion when he set you up to move ahead of God. If your vision seems to be tarrying, do not lose heart. You have God's Word that your vision will be realized in due season.

When I was a ten-year-old boy, my mother died, but God still had a plan for my life. While waiting in line as a teenager, I was afflicted with a crippling disease, but God still had a plan for my life. It would have been very easy for me to give up on God. It would have been very easy for me to get out of line. Thank God that I did not allow the enemy to abort God's plan for my life! God knew all along I was going to be a pastor, so He made sure I endured. Whatever you do, do not get out of line.

May I Have Your Order, Please?

Chapter Six
STILL WAITING?
SPECIAL ORDERS TAKE MORE TIME
(The Challenging Part of Life)

This chapter is very special to me, but I realize it is not for everybody. This chapter is for those people who have asked God for something different – something out of the ordinary.

Waiting can be difficult. Imagine how you feel when everyone behind you has gotten their orders filled, and you have had to pull over to the side and wait even longer. Waiting was not so bad when you were waiting with a group of folks, but now you are waiting by yourself and it seems like there is something wrong with that picture.

Just remember this: birds flock together, eagles soar alone.

As you continue to wait on your special order, God will reveal and develop what you really are – an eagle. Eagles do not struggle to fly; they, instead, use the resistance of the wind to sustain them. Eagles fly above the storm. Eagles do not live like chickens or other birds.

One restaurant had a popular slogan: "Special orders do not upset us." For those placing a special order, this statement simply is not true. When you want a burger without sauce or pickles, they cannot just give you a burger that has already been prepared. They have to make yours while you are waiting. If you are in a car with several other people and they want burgers prepared the usual way, then you might get some funny looks because now everyone has to wait because your order is different.

I can personally identify with special orders, because I placed a special order with God. I did not just want a church; I wanted a church with a bowling alley, a movie theater, an ice cream parlor, and an indoor running track. To top it off, I wanted to have it paid off in a short period of time.

You can imagine how many pastors passed me by while I was waiting in line. They had churches much sooner than I did. Truthfully, it made me have doubts when I continued to watch them get their churches. I had to remind myself that I had a special order.

Many times special orders take us by surprise. Imagine thinking your wait is over and that you are on your way to the final stop – the pickup window. As you make your approach, you can smell the fries. You can just imagine the taste of the Big Mac. You have waited so long. You kept your desire and stayed in line, and as a result, you are now about to receive your order.

You remind yourself as you approach, "Ask for ketchup and extra napkins." You pull up to the window, stick your hand out to receive your order, and to your surprise, the person looks at you and says, "Please pull up to the waiting area in front of the restaurant and we will bring your order out to you."

"What? Why? I've already paid and I've been in line a long time."

"Well," he or she replies, "it's because you ordered a Big Mac with no sauce, and because we do not make Big Macs without sauce, you have a special order...and special orders take more time."

There is no need to be angry, and no need to change your order. Just remind yourself that special orders just take more time.

Now comes the most challenging part of the journey – waiting. Get ready to park, turn off the engine, and let the kids hang their heads out of the window, because you will be here a while. This is where fifty percent of most Christians miss it. They fail to "wait" on God to answer their prayers.

You may ask, "You mean to tell me that everybody has to go through a period of waiting?"

Yes, everybody. And, those who want something different have a special waiting period.

In order to put everything in the proper perspective, you need to go back and look at what you ordered. Do not fuss because someone got his or her chicken before you got your steak. It takes longer to prepare steak than it does chicken. So the problem is not you or the restaurant help. It could be that what you are asking for is a special order.

A special order is when you ask God for a new house and you are only making five dollars an hour. You can get your house, but that is a special order. God has to spend some time getting the conditions right so you can afford it and that will take a little more time than a regular order. People all around you may get their blessings while you are waiting, but you just wait. God will come through for you, too.

What God ordains, He sustains. God is a God of peace and wholeness, lacking nothing. He is not going to provide your special order until you have the ability to handle it. Therefore, the delay is not to get your blessing ready, but to mature you so that you will be able to handle it.

If you are able to provide your blessing for yourself, it is not from God. You will not be able to do for yourself what God wants to do for you. God will have to work through you. Letting what God places in your hands control your heart means you are going in the wrong direction. The way you handle what God gives you determines your destiny.

Eagle-minded people must have high expectations. Expectation is visualizing what you are expecting. Most people do not receive because they do not expect to receive what they are waiting for. God has an appointed time for your blessing. Remember that it is God's idea for you to be blessed.

In the Old Testament we read:

"Then God blessed them, and God said to them, 'Be fruitful and multiply; fill the earth and subdue it; have dominion over the fish of the sea, over the birds of the air, and over every living thing that moves on the earth.'" (Genesis 1:28)

God has not changed. The God of Genesis is the God of Revelation. That is why we can have faith in Him. That is why we can trust Him to do what He says He will do.

Faith is expectancy that is released by your words and your actions. Faith and logic never get along. You have to live up to the prayer you have prayed.

It is like a woman giving birth to a baby. When the baby begins to push its way through the birth canal, the mother begins to dilate. To dilate means to expand or enlarge.

God has some big blessings for you, but your expectations, perhaps, are too low. Maybe you think He cannot give you those big blessings because your finances are too limited right now. But, God knows how to expand your finances and heighten your level of expectancy so He can bless you with what you asked for – but you will, possibly, have to wait a little longer.

Realize, too, that there can be stepping stones on the way to your order. You may want a two-hundred-thousand-dollar home, and God says you shall have what you say. But until He works out the conditions of your income, you may have to start out buying a fifty-thousand-dollar home. God says you can have your pink Mercedes-Benz, but your salary may only afford a Chevrolet right now. You may own several cars in between your Chevrolet and your Mercedes-Benz, but ultimately you get your dream car. God has to get your circumstances in order so that what you receive is a blessing to you and not a burden. God gives blessings, while Satan gives burdens. God will not give you anything that will cause you strain and worry. Starting out with a cashier's position does not mean that you will not own the store in the end. You are working your way up so that you not only get your blessing, but know how to keep it.

Those who place regular orders will pay for them, pick them up, and drive right past you. When it looks like everyone has received his or her blessing and you still have nothing, just remember that the preparation period is taking a little longer. Do not worry about what everybody else has, because God has something just for you. Knowing your "due season" helps ease frustration. God heard and filled your order when it was placed. The waiting process is for preparing you to receive it. It may cost you friends, time, ridicule, or discomfort, but in the end you win, as long as you do not get out of line.

I must admit that for a long time after we placed our order for a new church, it appeared that new churches were being built all around us. Even though our building would only hold about six hundred or seven hundred people, we remained diligent with four full services every Sunday. Believe it or not, we could not even accept new members because we did not have room for people to come down the aisle and give their lives to Christ. But, we did not get out of line. We just kept waiting – parked in the waiting area.

Patience is a Spiritual Force

You may have to wait so long in line that you almost lose the desire for your special order. I encourage you to stay in line and not lose heart, because you are closer to receiving your blessing than you have ever been. You need to practice "Spiritual Patience" while you are waiting.

Every believer has to run his or her own race. If your special order is a simple prayer request, quite naturally you can expect it to be delivered in a short period of time. That type of blessing is the equivalent of running a fifty-yard dash.

But, your one-of-a-kind, above average prayer request will take a longer period of time to be delivered. Your special order is the equivalent to running a marathon. You must possess the perseverance to not give up and the patience to endure. You must endure to the end, because at the end your special order from God awaits you. Remember that the longer you wait, the greater the reward.

> *"But let patience have her perfect work, that you may be perfect and entire, wanting nothing."*
> (James 1:4)

The Bible says that through faith and patience, we possess the promises of God. Have you ever been told to just have patience? It does not mean that you just sit down and allow things to come. Anybody can sit down and wait on something. Unfortunately, that is what most people think patience is – just sitting back and waiting. Patience, obviously, is much more than that. For the Christian, patience is an offensive weapon of spiritual warfare. Patience means to be constant or unchanging in your attitude, posture, and position toward what God has promised in His Word.

Imagine a bridge. A bridge has piers that help support it and hold it in place, right? Well, if faith is a bridge, then patience is the pier that supports it.

Many people say they have faith, and they do, until pressure is put on that faith. They have faith as long as they do not have to wait for an answer. As soon as they have a situation that requires waiting on God for an answer, they lack the patience to wait.

Some have faith as long as they know they have money in the bank, but once they have had to spend it all and have had to wait, they begin to think that there are no piers in the middle of their bridge. Faith must be accompanied by patience. Patience keeps faith intact, causing it to be constant throughout the trials and temptations you encounter.

Whatever the trial, faith supports your prayers – and patience supports your faith. Remember that as a Christian our problems are only opportunities for God to prove that His Word really works.

What if I were to tell you that from now until you die, you will never again have another problem? Would that make you feel wonderful? Of course, it would! But it would not be true. The truth is that you are going to have your share of problems.

And that might just be a blessing. Those problems could be just the thing you need to get you to your next level of faith. So, from this point on, change your perspective and begin to look at problems as God's opportunities to prove His power to you.

Dealing with a financial problem? That is God's opportunity to supply.

Feeling sick? That is God's opportunity to heal.

Feeling a little sad or depressed? That is God's opportunity to give joy.

God has a solution for every single thing that the world calls a problem. When you exercise your faith as a Christian, you are creating an atmosphere for God to provide a solution in a situation where a problem could exist.

Unfortunately, many Christians give up under the pressure of trials and never experience this truth. How many people do you know who have given up under the weight of a trial or temptation and gone back to the world? They missed the opportunity for God to work in their lives. They missed the opportunity to take God at His Word by exercising their faith and patience.

If you operate in faith and allow patience to come and have its perfect work, then you are going to be perfect and complete, wanting nothing.

Why?

Because you acted on God's Word and every trial is simply an opportunity to allow God to prove Himself to you. You are destined for victory.

Real faith is giving God the glory before you receive your blessing. While you are in line, do not allow yourself to look disillusioned and depressed. Here is the perfect opportunity for you to exercise your faith by praising God. He has already confirmed your special order through your confession and payment. So act like it. Thank Him for being faithful concerning His promises to you.

We did not realize that when we placed the order for a new church, God had already begun to fill our order by placing people in positions to bless us. We had no way of knowing that God was filling our order through some people operating out of Saint Louis, Missouri. I did not know them and they did not know me.

God also used a wonderful gentleman by the name of Edward Moore. I did not know him and he did not know me, but all the time God was preparing the hearts of these men to answer our prayer.

Many people might ask, "How could you want a racquetball court, arcade room, and billiards room in a church?"

I did not worry about such questions, because I knew it was God's responsibility to fill the order. My responsibility was to place the order, to have faith in God, and to wait.

There is ample Scripture to support God's promises, and to support His power in helping His people overcome every obstacle that stands in their way, but not everyone trusts God to deliver. For example:

> *"And they went and came to Moses, and to Aaron, and to all the congregation of the children of Israel, unto the wilderness of Paran, to Kadesh; and brought back word unto them, and unto all the congregation, and showed them the fruit of the land. And they told him, and said, 'We came unto the land whither thou sent us, and surely it flows with milk and honey; and this is the fruit of it. Nevertheless the people are strong that dwell in the land, and the cities are walled, and very great: and moreover we saw the children of Anak there. The Amalekites dwell in the land of the south: and the Hittites, and the Jebusites, and the Amorites, dwell in the mountains: and the Canaanites dwell by the sea, and by the coast of Jordan.' And Caleb stilled the people before Moses, and said, 'Let us go up at once, and possess it; for we are well able to overcome it."* (Numbers 13:26-30)

Of the twelve scouts who went into the Promised Land, only Caleb and Joshua brought back a favorable report in spite of what they saw. The people who were living there were giants, but to Caleb and Joshua they looked like grasshoppers. They both knew that in God's eyes, His children were the real giants.

In difficult situations, we need the spirit of Caleb and Joshua. They looked beyond impossible circumstances to accomplish God's purpose. Surround yourself with people who can see beyond visual range. Caleb had a "just do it" attitude. We need that same Caleb attitude. At the age of eighty-five, Caleb courageously took possession of the land and the neighboring hill country, driving out the giants who possessed it. Caleb recognized that he served a mighty God.

You either have faith or fear. Fear is false evidence that appears to be real. Bottom line: either you trust God or you do not. Here are some key points that will help build your confidence and trust in God:

- You can let go and let God, because God knows what He is doing.

- Your success is God's problem, not yours.

- When you do what you can, God will do what you cannot.

- The Holy Spirit is your helper and constant companion.

- You do not have to know it all, but you do have to know God.

- Your part is to plant the seed; God's part is to grow the seed.

- God will never disappoint you.

- Things run a lot smoother when you make it easy on yourself and harder on God.

- Life has not passed you by; it is all in front of you.

- The Lord is still working on you; He is not yet finished with you.

Having lost one million nine hundred thousand dollars, we were facing great opposition. We needed God to answer us by a certain time. We had to realize that no matter how impossible the circumstances appear, God will make a way. God does not have a "Plan B," only a "Plan A." To create a secondary course of action indicates that there is some degree of doubt, apprehension, or margin of error in the original plan. God has everything planned out, down to the hour, minute, and second.

Whether it takes fifteen years, six months, or two hours, everything God has promised you in His Word is yours. Once you realize it and get a taste of victory, you will never again settle for defeat. If you follow God's plan for receiving blessings, you can and will always have a sweat-free victory.

When you are waiting on God to do something and you have run out of "wait," God gives you more "wait." To wait on the Lord means to serve God with praise, worship, and adoration. You are like a waiter in a restaurant who is serving a customer. When a waiter does an exceptional job of serving, the customer is motivated to leave a tip.

Serve with gladness, waiting day after day, month after month, and year after year, keeping a smile on your face and praise in your heart. God knows that you are serving Him with gladness – and when He blesses you, He will give you a tip. In fact, God will throw a little something extra in with your blessing.

Our church had a special order and, while waiting on God, we continued to serve the Lord with gladness. We praised and worshipped Him even when we did not see any signs that He was answering our prayers.

I believe that when you serve God with praise and worship, He is motivated to tip you, and I mean He's going to tip you generously. How does He tip you? He will give you something extra that you did not know you needed.

God gives you strength from the inside, which enables you to override what you feel or what you are going through. There is a miracle on the other side, but you must go through. Faith is not based on feelings, but on the Word of God. If you have God's Word, that is all you need. God has promised you that His Word will not return to Him void.

God will take you through things to make you wait. The most powerful things are happening inside of you while you are waiting. Waiting on a particular level will increase your strength and help you maintain at the promised level.

The devil knows that when the Word is taught, if you as the hearer take it and sow it into your heart, then you will be better, stronger, and more fruitful. What the devil hopes is that you will forget what you have been taught before you have a chance to act on it. The Word of God is sown into your heart each time you hear a sermon. You must also sow the Word into your heart on a daily basis by reading the Word for yourself. Do not allow Satan to steal it by affliction and persecution.

Your praise of God silences the devil. Such praise keeps him from attacking you through your emotions, your body, or your mind. God wants you to praise Him before you place your order, while you are waiting on your order, and after you receive your order.

Satan will attack your mind. If he can get in your mind, he can change your behavior. Your focus on God is essential because there is a constant battle over who and what is going to control you.

Will you stand and fight with the weapon God has given you, or will you succumb to Satan's attacks? Remember to praise and continue to focus on the promises and benefits of His Word. Whatever circumstances or situations you encounter in your life, continue to thank God. In everything give thanks.

You cannot look at what is; look at what is supposed to be. Do not focus on what you see.

Get Planted

"Blessed is the man that walks not in the counsel of the ungodly, nor stands in the way of sinners, nor sits in the seat of the scornful. But his delight is in the law of the Lord; and in His law does he meditate day and night. And he shall be like a tree planted by the rivers of water, that brings forth his fruit in his season; his leaf also shall not

wither; and whatsoever he does shall prosper."
(Psalm 1:1-3)

A blessed man does not just wait – he is planted. God plants the feet of those who are blessed. Blessings do not just happen. They come to you because you make a decision to be planted.

You were planted at a specific time and specific place to wait on God to manifest blessings in your life. Who would have thought that you would be willing to invest so much time in waiting on God to deliver your order? God is allowing this time to allow your faith to grow deeper, to get your roots down.

All the storms during your waiting period strengthened your faith. Most people wait as long as it seems easy, but if it appears as if there is going to be some opposition, they change their minds. In such cases, it is not that God has not blessed you, but you moved from where God meant for you to be. Do not get out of line; stay planted.

You must be rooted in God's Word. The first step is joining an anointed ministry where the Word is going forth on a constant basis. When you pray, be honest with God. He already knows. Learn to renew your mind daily with the word of God. Submit to following the Holy Spirit, Who is sent to lead and guide you. When you mess up, which you will, repent so that the devil cannot make you walk in condemnation. And, most of all – be consistent in your daily walk with God.

Blessings are positional and seasonal. You must be in position to receive. We must live in a posture of receiving. God blesses those who are expecting to be blessed. God's Word will guide you to wherever He is sending your blessing.

The devil will try to send storms to uproot you from where God would have you wait. Those storms will come in many shapes and forms. Storms can be family, finances, health, and emotional turmoil. You must realize that whatever storm Satan sends your way, God built you with that storm in mind.

God's Word says He knew you before He placed you in your mother's womb. God equipped you with everything you would need before you drew your first breath.

Suppose you are driving a car on a beautiful sunny day and suddenly it begins to rain. Do you take the car back to the dealership and request that windshield wipers be installed? No, because the car is already equipped with windshield wipers. It was equipped before you bought it. The car manufacturer knew the potential owner would not always have sunny weather for driving, so the car was equipped for all types of weather conditions.

God is your manufacturer. Nothing catches Him off guard. He knew exactly what you would need to face the storms in your life, so He equipped you with everything needed to weather them.

There are some things He has placed within you that you are not even aware of. God has made you storm-proof. The storm will come to uproot and move you out of position. Stand and do not move. He will answer your prayer, but you have to be there. God built you with your special order in mind.

People who are planted grow. The roots of a blessed man grow down before they grow up. You must get your roots down before your flower comes forth. God is more concerned with how deep your roots go down than with how far your branches spread. You are only concerned about receiving your blessing, but God is concerned about your life. You are a piece of the Master – and that makes you a masterpiece.

Sometimes the delay in your order is intentional so that God can show you His glory. In the Bible, a rich ruler named Jairus came to Jesus and asked Him to heal his daughter. Before Jesus arrived, she died. The man immediately thought healing was now impossible, and so did his family and friends. However, Jesus raised his daughter after the delay to show Jairus and his family and friends that it is not over until God says it is over.

Sometimes it takes an event like this to show you that there are times when your situation has to appear dead before it can be resurrected. Never speak doubt. What you tend to say is what you tend to do. Doubt will come, but never speak it. Doubt confessed is doubt possessed. Doubt is the greatest enemy to the Word of God because it keeps you from operating in faith. When doubt comes, ignore it.

Hope without faith is nothing. Hope should always set the goal. Hope keeps you alive. Hope will let you smile while the ship is sinking, but faith keeps the ship afloat.

You have got to fake it until you make it.

Your demeanor should always confuse the devil. When people see you waiting for your special order, they should see a person confident in his posture and positive in his words. It is a matter of your countenance versus your circumstances. Once your roots are firmly planted, you become like a tree planted by the water. Whatever you do will prosper.

During the planting process, you will exercise much prayer, a lot of crying, fasting, and giving. Now, having done all, as the Word says, you qualify to stand and watch God move.

> "*Hope deferred makes the heart sick: but when the desire comes, it is a tree of life*" (Proverbs 13:12).

In all honesty, when our blessing takes a long time, we tend to wonder if God really wants us to have it. When the thing we are hoping for is delayed, we may begin to feel a little weary. But, remember that delay is not denial.

Though your heart may feel sick during the delay, know that the blessings of God belong to you. God sees you looking denied. God sees you looking rejected. He knows when you are at your end and at just the right time, everything you ever prayed and hoped for will be manifested.

Faith is an action. It requires that you act on what you believe before you ever see it. If you see it, it is not faith.

Faith is always present tense. God is a "now" God. You do not ever run out of faith. You must believe that what will be already is. Your circumstances are not beyond God's ability.

In a classroom, when a test is in progress, the teacher is silent. When you are standing on the promises of God and it seems as if your prayer is not being answered, you may be in a period of testing. This time is not for God to embarrass you or alienate you, but to determine what you have learned.

For example, in a classroom a student has the opportunity to ask as many questions as he or she wants in order to understand the subject. A good teacher will answer those questions and develop a relationship with the student. The teacher's primary objective is to prepare the student for test time. During test time there are no questions. The student must apply what he has learned.

When God is silent, your test is in progress. Remember that the greater the delay, the greater the reward. The Word says, *"But when it comes it is a tree of life."* When what you hoped for is manifested, it brings great joy. It brings increased trust and stronger faith in God to know that the *whatsoever things* you have asked for have been given to you.

If it seems like you have been waiting for so long that you have been forgotten, do not worry. God has angels watching over you. When you have waited long enough, someone is going to knock on your car window and hand you your order.

We cannot appreciate abundance until we have endured a season of drought. God wants you to be a good steward of your special order. God does not need additional time to prepare a special order for you, but in His wisdom He is preparing you for the special order.

During this time, God enlarges your heart. He enlarges your capacity to love and be loved. When God knows He can trust you with a blessing and that you can share it with others, just as Jesus did, your special order will manifest.

There Is No Testimony Without a Test

After about a year of waiting, our prayers began to manifest. We started to actually see evidence of what God was doing. A banker from Missouri who was reading our web page on the Internet called me and said, "Hey, how are you guys doing?"

I did not know this man and had never seen him before, but I said, "Well, I do not know how we are doing, but we are trying to build a new church."

He said, "I'm coming to Dallas and I want to talk to you, because I'm really impressed with what your ministry is doing."

He flew here from Saint Louis, and we went to dinner and fellowshipped. We discussed some of the wonderful things God was doing for us. It was not long before he asked, "How much money do you need?"

I told him we needed six million dollars. We needed five million dollars by the following Thursday or the church we had a contract on would be sold to someone else.

Two days before the deadline, we received a check for five million dollars. We went to the closing, paid the money, and got the church.

It is not that God was getting our money ready; the money was already there. God had to get us ready. We received our special order.

Once in the new building, God continued to bless us, and our church family continued to grow. It was not long before I was taking a plane out of town to inform the bankers that the building they had blessed us with the finances to purchase was no longer big enough.

As a result of learning to wait and to not get out of line, we now have that ice cream parlor, full-sized gymnasium, game room, and racquetball court. We now have that movie theater, playstation room, and video arcade. We have the billiards room, gym, fitness track, bridal parlor, and bowling alley. We also have two full-service schools in our building.

But, more important, we have a place to worship together as a church family. As a tip for having waited for our special order, God blessed us with three thousand, three hundred and thirty-nine new members in one year. We asked for a church and He gave us a facility that was bigger and more beautiful than we could ever have imagined.

I am not writing these things to brag, but to empower you. Knowledge is power. Through my writings and God's Word, I have tried to give you the tools to get what I have gotten.

The Bible clearly tells us that God is no respecter of persons, and that what He did for me He will also do for you. I want you to know that He answers prayers. God is bigger than your problems. He is greater than your dreams, and He will answer your prayers if you will just trust Him.

During the waiting process, there are some valuable lessons to be learned that you can only learn by waiting. Special orders can be challenging, but they allow us to capture all that God has for us. I could have had just a church, but I wanted to bless the people of God with a facility that would meet a lot of their needs.

As Christians, we talk about places in the world, but if we do not provide ourselves with these places in a spiritual setting, where else will our people go? The young people in my church can have a pizza party, watch movies, and never have to leave the church.

Waiting is not necessarily a bad thing. As a result of waiting, we received increased strength and a deeper abiding faith in our Father. I am the first to admit that getting through the process to the promise is not easy, but I would do it all over again just to see God work it out.

You will need to read some of the chapters in this book over and over again until you get them in your spirit. Once you get them in your spirit, you will be unstoppable! You will actually be able to see yourself go to another level in your spiritual life.

Your special order is really not about you. Like the miracles in the Bible, your special order is to show others what God can do through your life and your situations so that they will seek Him and want to draw closer to Him. That is why it is so important to give God all the glory for the manifestation of your blessings.

No matter how much I share with you, there is nothing I can say that will actually give you the joy of having your own order filled. Picking up your order is the most rewarding part of life. Not only does it bless you, it blesses all those around you. Hopefully the people around you joined you in prayer and watched you through every step of the process of receiving your blessing. Your testimony of how God worked in your life will undoubtedly strengthen them.

So do not be afraid to dream big. Do not worry about what others may say about your order. Carefully look over the menu to make sure you are willing to pay the price for what you want. Make sure that you are willing to wait in line as long as it will take. Then, proceed to the menu board to place your order.

Remember: God is already at the menu board waiting for you, and He has one simple question: "May I have your order, please?"

ABOUT THE AUTHOR

Pastor Rickie G. Rush has proven over the years that a humble heart and an inspiring word will allow you to have many followers. The Dallas preacher has grown his ministry from a faithful flock of nine to a flourishing congregation of more than fourteen thousand.

Rush has won the love of many because he has labored among them. He started his career as an instructor in the Dallas Independent School District at Skyline High School, where he himself attended school. As a teacher, Rush not only taught students, he mentored them and molded them. He developed a mutual rapport and respect with them that has continued over the years. Rush still keeps up with many of his students and receives countless letters about the successes in their lives.

However, it has been Rush's uncanny ability to handle troubled teens that has brought him to the spotlight whenever and wherever there is a youth crisis. His youthful magnetism has brought young people from throughout the Dallas- Fort Worth metroplex to join his church. His congregation has one of the largest youth memberships in the area, with a "Prayer Posse" which consists of more than three hundred young people from the ages of twelve to nineteen.

Although Rush has had many successes and is becoming nationally known for his growing ministry, those who know him understand that he comes from a very humble beginning. Rush started his preaching career when only ten years of age, following the tragic loss of his mother.

Yet, it was Rush's near-brush with death in the late seventies from Guillain-Barre Syndrome that changed his outlook on life. In his late teens, he suddenly found himself combating this life-threatening disease which attacks the central nervous system. During his two-year battle with this illness, he was paralyzed and comatose for two months of this period.

Rush recovered with a vengeance and with a determination that would not let anything stop him. From his illness, he developed a new lease on life and an inner energy that has caused everything that he has touched to flourish. Rush paid for his multi-million dollar church facility in two years. He has also achieved numerous awards and accolades.

Rush earned his Bachelor of Arts degree from the University of Texas at Arlington and has a Doctor of Divinity Degree from Rialto Bible College.

However, people do not look to Rush for his academic accomplishments, but rather for his ability to reach the everyday person. He is not resting on his laurels. He is pulling together everything he has learned to empower believers through a straightforward and unique book, which draws on his experience with prayer.

In this, his first book, Rush shares the step-by-step process of how to properly apply faith to move from the realm of praying "glass-ceiling prayers" to a fervent and effectual prayer life of getting all that God has for you.

His book, **May I Have Your Order, Please?,** helps you release your prayer power to position you for the ultimate blessing from God.

Rush is renowned for his ability to inspire people of all ages, while teaching the basic principles of God's Word. His book, sermons, and lectures often include colorfully illustrated memories of growing up on welfare in the impoverished projects of West Dallas, Texas.

Today, the Rev. Dr. Rickie G. Rush resides in Dallas with his family. He currently serves as pastor of the Inspiring Body of Christ Church in Dallas, Texas. The Inspiring Body of Christ Church (IBOC) is a multi-cultural, non-denominational church with the primary mission of winning lost souls to Christ.

May I Have Your Order, Please?

In order to book Pastor Rickie G. Rush for speaking engagements or book signings, please contact:

Inspiring Body of Christ Church Worldwide Ministries
7710 South Westmoreland Road
Dallas, Texas 75237

Church Phone:
972-572-4262 (IBOC)

Church Fax:
972-709-3888

Notes

To: Tina Miller

*I <u>Know</u> that you are in heaven, and
I believe that you will always be standing
right behind me.*

Your little pastor,
Rickie G. Rush